1999

Wright

Iohn
Wright

Guido
Fawkes

Robert
Catesby

THE
GUNPOWDER
PLOT

The gunpowder plot was immediately fixed in the collective memory of the English people by engravings (some more clumsy than this), sermons, prayers, bonfires, bell-ringing and even, at a later date, licensed puppet shows

THE
GUNPOWDER
PLOT
FAITH IN REBELLION

Alan Haynes

SUTTON PUBLISHING

First published in 1994 by
Sutton Publishing Limited · Phoenix Mill · Thrupp
Stroud · Gloucestershire

Paperback edition first published in 1996

A catalogue record of this book is available from the British Library

ISBN 0-7509-1246-4

Cover illustration: Engraving of the plotters by a Dutch artist (Photograph: The Mansell Collection)

Typeset in 11/12 Ehrhardt
Typesetting and origination by
Sutton Publishing Limited
Printed in Great Britain by
WBC Limited, Bridgend

Contents

In loving memory of my parents

Eve and William Haynes

Acknowledgements

My thanks are due to a number of people for information and advice, including Brian Bonnard, Ralph B. Weller, Timothy Morris, and Charles Nicholl, who took time from his current project to read the whole book. I am especially grateful to Dr Mark Nicholls, Department of Manuscripts and University Archives, Cambridge University Library, for doing the same; and to Claude Blair for answering so fully a naïve enquiry about swords. The result was a great surprise to both of us (see Appendix II). Once again the Hélène Heroys Literary Foundation (Switzerland) has supported my work with a generous financial donation when nothing was offered by any English source.

Photographs were supplied by, or are reproduced by, kind permission of the following: Courtauld Institute; Huntington Library, San Marino, Cal.; Mansell Collection; Schweizerisches Landes museum (Zurich); Weiss Gallery, London; and the Worshipful Company of Mercers, London.

God forbid that we should give
out a dream of our own imagination
for a pattern of the world.

Francis Bacon

In conjectures I durst not be too bold,
but when they seem to offer themselves,
they deserve the choice of judgment.

John Selden

ONE

The Politics of Salvation

It was a defensive and angry King Henry VIII with his compliant ministers, clerics and a complacent Parliament who had snatched the English church from papal control. In the years after this sensational event, the struggle for the soul of England and Wales was conducted variously with dignity, acrimony and cunning cruelty, as well as raging conviction. Religion remained 'the motive power of the age'. The puzzled and beleaguered English Catholic community of clerics and laymen struggled to find a secure place in a challenging, discordant Protestant society in which some Protestant reformers heaped scorn on Catholicism calling the Catholic Church 'the Pope's playhouse' and endeavouring to prove that the pontiffs had in the later ages fulfilled the prophecy of St John in regard to the Antichrist. The chronological and historical sense of identity and obligation became severely distorted. The Elizabethan calendar year for the Church, law and government began late in March, generally coinciding with the major festival of Easter and the timeless, visible hope of spring. Popular usage continued to call 1 January 'new year's day'. Protestants and puritans alike shifted their religious observance away from the quotidian cycles of the land and the old liturgical cycle, because they lived in towns and there were clocks to rival bells. The disconnection had profound consequences. 'The Protestants took upon themselves in different spirits the robes of the prophets.'[1] For those of the old faith an arhythmic and unnatural tugging at the spirit took place, engendering simultaneous feelings of belonging and estrangement. These were especially disturbing for the lesser peerage and gentry class of landowners; from the Humber to the Severn there stretched a solid belt of opulent and obstinate followers of the old religion.

Pressure on Catholics was immediate under Elizabeth since the religious settlement effected by and for her in 1559–60, which smothered the flames of Protestant martyrs, also completed the 'institutional wreckage begun with the monasteries, advanced by the chantries acts and furthered by the conversions of the priesthood'. Even a mild resistance to this was hard to muster after the crashing failure in 1569 of the rebellion of the northern earls of Northumberland and Westmorland. From then on, Catholicism, like a great lake subject to a newly hostile climate, began to shrink to areas remote from London and the privy council, to country villages, sometimes to just a great seigneurial house and its environs, where observation and obligation fast tethered it. Lord Vaux made the point in 1581 when he claimed that his house had become his parish.[2] The rituals

All the plots against Elizabeth I and her government failed, and the spies employed by her councillors helped in the defeat of enemies at home and abroad

of the old faith could be conducted indoors with some trepidation, but public expressions of it were normally held to be too risky. Even so, there were those for whom its importance overrode disquiet at the possible consequences. The Rookwoods in Suffolk, for example, kept Corpus Christi, the greatest feast of the late medieval church, with great solemnity and music 'and the day of the Octave made a solemn procession about a great garden',[3] but ventured no further. The most unhappy pendant to the woeful failure in 1569, and the fierce government repression that then followed, on the instigation of William Cecil, Lord Burghley, was the insidious growth of self-pity. This erratic growth could lead to a lack of realism as the government pressed their advantage and devised an auxiliary policy of seeking to impoverish Catholics materially. As their wealth was gnawed away, so too was their chief spiritual resource – the priesthood. Out of this dismal jam of oppression and self-repression (a key component in the growth of a conspiracy) came elements of resistance and among the clerics in exile there was the notable Dr (later Cardinal) William Allen to give voice and funds to their efforts. His initial leanings to Protestantism had been swamped and he regarded the Elizabethan Settlement as an affront to believers.[4] When he at length founded the English College at Douai in Flanders it was 'so that English seminarians could return home to gentry households, primarily in London and the Thames valley where Catholicism was not the strongest, in order to provide pastoral care and, in some cases, engage in soul-saving.' Since the gentry household was a supportive institution for an extended 'family' of blood relations and servants, the government saw no option but to apply pressure. The looming problem was now to extirpate Catholicism by statute without provoking a sequence of bloody stirs that would have to be put down with rigour. It was a problem given another twist by the maverick presence in England of a Catholic claimant to the English throne – Mary, Queen of Scots. Moreover, the end of the rebellion in 1569 had not been instantly achieved, and the government doubtless reflected ruefully on their good fortune that the earls were incompetents.

Nor had their external sympathizers proved much wiser, it has to be said, and the publication of the papal bull *Regnans in Excelsis* (25 February 1570) confirmed this. The purity of intention of Pope Pius V need not be doubted for he had a mode of thinking unblemished by low political considerations. He held Elizabeth to be an open, avowed heretic, who had broken her solemn promise, and all that was necessary was this bull which would restore the faith. It excommunicated her from the Roman Catholic Church without warning because of her manifestations of heresy, and it immediately deposed her from the throne without the usual formal delay of one year following excommunication. The people were hence released from obligation or allegiance to this ruler and commanded to flout her laws. Even without a clear call to Catholics to rebel, such risings as happened were condoned, so encouraging those who previously might have held back from such an extreme tactic. So the bull polarized domestic matters in an international context when it was made public in England by John Felton, the Catholic barrister who nailed it to the door of the Bishop of London's residence in a wry parody of Luther. It suggested to many 'that patriotism could not permit them to follow so extreme a religion'. But others recoiled because if they took the Pope at his word it was likely that they too would die like Felton on the gallows. Papal support of the Ridolfi plot against Elizabeth was equally ill-advised; the vision of a saint in the making in Rome did no harm for the time being to Mary Stuart, but her ally the Duke of Norfolk was tried and executed in 1572.[5]

It is worth recalling that in its particulars the Elizabethan Settlement never had been lenient. To accelerate acceptance and flush out dissenters a parliamentary statute was passed in the spring of 1563. Known as *An Act for the assurance of the Queen's Majesty's royal power* . . . it was directed 'against those that extol the power of the Bishop of Rome and refuse the oath of allegiance'. The dilemma for Catholics was underscored by the retributive element: on the first refusal to take the oath they were liable to loss of lands and imprisonment, and a second refusal was regarded as treason and punishable by death. After the 1569 rebellion, which had so shaken confidence, the government issued Queen Elizabeth's *Defense of Her Proceedings in Church and State* which outlined her authority in the Church. It made claims for royal authority that were modest when compared to the statements of her father, while still declaring the intention to oversee 'the laws of God and man which are ordained to that end to be duly observed, and the offenders against the same duly punished . . .'. New legislation was passed in 1571 by Elizabeth's third Parliament. In the Treasons statute there was a direct borrowing of a phrase from the earlier statute of 1534 which prohibited any speech of writing that labelled the monarch a 'heretic, schismatic, tyrant, infidel or an usurper' – all things that the more reckless of the animated disciples of Mary Stuart were liable to example. To buttress the statute there was now a prohibition on spoken words or texts that denied Elizabeth's lawful occupation of the throne. A second statute made the attempt to execute a papal bull treason, as was any attempt to lure to Rome anyone willing to jettison their obedience to the queen. The third statute was directed against the property of Catholic exiles, especially those who had scattered after the disaster of late 1569 – the rebellion being followed by summary trials and many executions.

In the mid-1570s the effort of William Allen at Douai, then Rheims and later Rome, in the English colleges for seminarians, began to mature. The clandestine return to England of enthusiastic young priests in disguise led to some gains, but the grip of the government remained severe. Nor was there anyone among the opposition with sufficient political weight to negotiate for toleration of dissident religion, and with the secret arrival of the first Jesuit mission a new and unnerving political component was suddenly thrust into the exchanges. It was assumed that the provisions of *Regnans in Excelsis* had a meaning beyond the papal court, especially in Spain, which was set on a course of expansion, absorbing Portugal by force of arms and threatening to crush the Dutch rebels. Remove practical leadership or block its growth and the void is inevitably filled by heedless enthusiasts (like, later, the young Lenin) whose prescriptions are moulded by fanaticism. Such a man at the end of the sixteenth century was Father Robert Persons (or Parsons) of the Society of Jesus who mesmerized the eager and impressionable after returning to England in company with Father Edmund Campion and others.[6] Persons was a yeoman's son and scholarship boy whose formidable abilities had allowed him to better himself. The former fellow and dean of Balliol College, Oxford, was as covertly political as any Jesuit was allowed to be by the rules of the order. The *Instructions* to the returners said that they were not to become involved in affairs of state, nor write to Rome about political matters, nor speak, nor allow others to speak in their presence, against the queen – except perhaps with those whose fidelity had been long and steadfast, and even then not without strong reasons.

Still, the agenda of the Jesuits was not a mystery.[7] They intended the reversal of Protestant gains and capitulation to Rome, and though Edmund Campion, whose covert preaching aroused such tender admiration and fervour, might be regarded as less obviously political than Persons, he belonged to an order that was meshed with the enemies of England, and the Spanish party, supported by Persons as an active and able member, did not confine itself entirely to writings. In order to defeat the Jesuit mission which was noted by English spies of the privy council even before the covert landing in England, the government set out new legislation in the third session of the fourth Elizabethan Parliament: two anti-Catholic measures 'to make provision of laws more strict and more severe' in order to force them 'to yield their open obedience'. The bill introduced by Sir Francis Knollys, father-in-law of the Earl of Leicester whose puritanism had an increasingly political slant, raised the fine for absence from Sunday communion from 1s. to a startling and potentially ruinous £20 per lunar month. This put pressure on the gentry of whom Burghley was most suspicious, and it met his demand for a weapon against 'the socially influential and politically dangerous'. It became treason to convert anyone to Catholicism, and even to be present at mass meant a year's imprisonment as well as a fine. To ensure that the Act worked as intended informers were rewarded. The second measure stiffened penalties for seditious words and rumours spoken against Elizabeth, with a second offence leading to execution. It was also made a felony to write or print material regarding the possible longevity of the queen and the acutely interesting matter of the succession. Even the puritans in the House of Commons flinched at this since they wondered if the government had them in its sights as well.

Meanwhile, Burghley was concerned with hunting down the Jesuits, particularly Campion who declared mildly he had come to preach the faith and not as an agent of the papacy to meddle in politics. The challenge for the energetic Persons was to do his work and evade all efforts to take him by scampering from one hideout to another. He succeeded triumphantly, but Campion was less fortunate and was eventually seized at the Yate family home, Lyford Grange in Berkshire. This was the result of the persistent efforts of a pursuivant George Eliot – known as 'Judas'. After a spell in the Little Ease in the Tower of London (a cell that cramped the body as well as the spirit by restricting movement), Campion was subjected to several examinations, including one by Elizabeth herself and another by ecclesiastical commissioners.[8] He was willing to defer to the queen's temporal power – she was his 'lawful governess' – but he must pay to God what was his, including the supremacy of the Church, a view that he maintained with sublime conviction after torture on the rack. On trial with the absent Allen and Persons (who had taken refuge at Michelgrove in Sussex, the home of the Shelley family, before taking a boat to exile), charged with a cluster of crimes against the state, Campion pleaded not guilty. Evidence against him was woefully thin, but he was still convicted by the jury under the terms of the Treason statute of 1352, because the government did not want the trial to slide into a forum for debate on the relationship 'between political allegiance and religious conversion'. It was difficult after Campion's execution on 1 December to brand him as a traitor – to many he was a martyr and Burghley thought it necessary to counter this with a special publication after the capture of Francis Throckmorton, and the discovery of Somerville's plan in the same year to assassinate Elizabeth. He developed his views (and those of the government) in the ominously titled pamphlet *The Execution of Justice in England* (1583) in which he affirmed 'the states right to take whatever measures it thought necessary in its own defence'. Only if England could be isolated from the phenomenon called the Counter-Reformation (and martyrs for the Church were martyrs for the Pope and his allies), would Catholicism in England be effectively held up and then stifled. As it has been pointed out by a biographer of Burghley, where political Catholicism was concerned he was ruthless because he was fighting for the survival of the Tudor realm, but somewhat surprisingly he was also capable of charity towards recusants as the leading Catholic Sir Thomas Tresham noted in his own correspondence with him.[9]

Powerfully loyal to Elizabeth, Lord Burghley liked modestly to claim that 'he had gotten more by his patience than ever he did by his wit'. We can disagree

Both Father Persons and Dr Allen responded to Burghley's pamphlet, the former also using the opportunity to attack another privy councillor, the Earl of Leicester, in a lengthy diatribe published in 1584 and known under the short title of *Leicester's Commonwealth*. Copies began to appear in England in the autumn of that year after the text had been assembled by a group of English lay Catholic exiles in France, with abundant help from Persons who organized its distribution from his bases in Rouen and Paris. In September Ralph Emerson, one of Persons' aides, for the second time smuggled copies into England before being arrested and committed to the Counter prison in Poultry Street. Leicester's self-esteem was wounded by the vitriolic text and he soon persuaded the privy council that it was not merely a personal squib aimed at his public and private reputation, but, more insidiously, an attack on the regime. However, the main effort to refute Burghley came in Allen's *A True, Sincere and Modest Defense of English Catholics*, which reiterated the claim that the prosecution of Catholics was actually for religous reasons; they suffered death only for 'cogitations and inward opinions' and 'never took arms in all England upon the bull of Pius V'. Against this the government was able, through its spy clusters and agents provocateurs, to offer apparent evidence that Allen was lying.

The shock of the Throckmorton plot with its links to Mary, Queen of Scots, the Pope and Philip II had been strong. The assassination of Prince William of Orange, leader of the Dutch patriots, added a further layer of distress and anger, since Leicester had long been advocating armed intervention to assist him. In October 1584 he and Burghley formed the Bond of Association which allowed the gentlemen who took the oath freedom to kill anyone who came to the English throne following the assassination of Elizabeth.[10] It was an emotional piece of propaganda since in effect it sanctioned civil war, but it remains understandable given the lowering atmosphere that had settled over the country. In addition the government decided to hammer the clandestine Jesuits again, and, like the proclamation of January 1581, the main item in the new bill made the presence of a Jesuit or seminary priest, whatever his purpose, a treasonable offence. It became a felony to succour them, and anyone with knowledge of their presence who did not inform against them incurred a fine and imprisonment. All the queen's subjects being educated abroad were to return home within six months and take the oath of supremacy – thus denying his Catholicism – while those who failed to do this incurred the penalties of treason. Not everyone in Parliament was entirely at ease with such draconian measures, but still the bill became law early in 1585, despite the willingness of some of the Catholic gentry to declare their allegiance to Elizabeth. Nor did these measures lie idle as many previous pieces of law-making had done; enforcement became the rule and in the next three years or so some 120 people were condemned by the statute.

Yet among the Catholic gentry there were still those who were not to be cowed by such battering legislation. The wealthy squire's son, Anthony Babington, had been distributing Catholic books, supporting the new Catholic clergy and sheltering priests even before he took up the cause of the exiled and imprisoned Mary, Queen of Scots, who symbolized for young men of his ilk their stricken and unfortunate faith.[11] Mariolatry had two sides, and her lambency became even

To most Protestant Elizabethans there was no contemporary of Elizabeth I more vexatious than Mary, Queen of Scots – meddlesome, mendacious and stupid

stronger after the execution of Campion and the enforcement of the recusancy laws 'had brought home to them the bitterness of their sufferings, which in royal patience she shared and surpassed'. Indeed, it has even been suggested that if Mary had been a Protestant the conspiracies on her behalf would have occurred just the same, because then the aim would have been simply a change of ruler, not a change of religion (and ruler). Young men of a romantic or chivalrous cast of mind then were often responsive to the somewhat obvious pathos of her dim situation; a peculiar misfortune, as it happened, since it could lead them into conflict with a swarm of spies and intelligencers reporting to Elizabeth's severe and puritan-inclined spy master, Sir Francis Walsingham. Given his position in the government as Secretary of State they were right to be frightened of him and his aides, yet they persisted with a passion in their sword-hilt protestations of loyalty to Mary, a tall woman with an interesting personal history. This devotion lodged itself in the core of the strike against Elizabeth first envisaged by John Ballard, the bustling exiled priest who easily and convincingly disguised himself as a soldier. Babington was initially reluctant to get involved, but when his feelings about it shifted and the plan began to evolve, it is possible to see a shadowy prefiguring of the gunpowder plot itself. Both plots were held together by a strongly felt male bond that could override the loyalties of marriage and fatherhood. For example, young Thomas Salusbury, the owner of Lleweni in North Wales and a gentleman in the service of his guardian, the Earl of Leicester, was devoted (for no clear reason) to Babington. Salusbury had been forced into a marriage when aged ten to his stepfather's daughter, an arrangement intended to secure financial advantages, and it was some years before he was reconciled to his bride.[12] Beside Salusbury in the taverns of London, where gentlemen (perhaps at

For twenty years the Secretary of State, Sir Francis Walsingham, risked his own health and comfort to serve his country

the Inns of Court) met for conviviality, was the young Welsh squire Edward Jones of Plas Cadwgan. He seems to have been an uncritical admirer of his compatriot whose style of clothes and beard marked him out as something of an exquisite, like the nonchalant and elegant young man in Nicholas Hilliard's portrait miniature *Young Man among Roses*. Even so, Salusbury gave Jones only passing attention being altogether taken with Babington, whose charm like that of Robert Catesby, was ultimately fatal. Another who centred his life on Babington was the minor poet Chidiock Tichborne, as did to a less marked degree John Travers and Edward Abington (sometimes given as Habington) whose fortunate brother Thomas managed to escape the brutal denouement of both the Babington and gunpowder plots. Was this because the second plot unravelled so sweetly for the government through the effect of the famous anonymous letter to Lord Monteagle, which one writer has ascribed to the pen of his lordship's sister Mary – the wife of Thomas Abington?

The more dangerous of the two plots was certainly Catesby's, because unlike the somewhat naïve Babington, who was compromised virtually at all points by government spies, he managed to exclude them. Still the similarities are striking for both men saw their efforts develop with the support of swordsmen with reputations as such, preliminary to a specific localized reaction in the country. For Babington this was intended to be the release of Mary, Queen of Scots and the gift of another crown and country to her. For Catesby, the culmination of his plot would come after the detonation of the gunpowder and would take place around Stratford-upon-Avon, with a general insurrection and a new government. At the head of this was to be placed the young Princess Elizabeth who at that time was also living in Warwickshire – at Combe Abbey, some four or five miles east of Coventry. In the case of neither man is it now possible to state with absolute certainty down to the last detail in what degree he shared his full plans with his supporters. In Babington's case this may well have been due to a clumsy effort to throw off the government; in sociopath Catesby's, to dissembling rooted in unconsidered, even anarchic, ambition. Perhaps he thought he could transform the former errors into positive action and so manufacture a triumph.

One of the secondary but not negligible effects of the Babington plot was to infuriate the Earl of Leicester. This was unfortunate for Catholics since in that frame of mind, as he proved repeatedly, he could be a very troublesome enemy. He had been trying for months to give the Dutch rebels direct support after they had sought the assistance of Elizabeth following the unexpected deaths of Prince William and François, Duke of Anjou. Leicester had been stuck in the Low Countries, piling up errors, both civil and military, during the period when Babington's plot was taking place. While Burghley and Walsingham could point to a sharp demolition of treason, he had managed to upset Elizabeth by his blunders abroad. Back in England to rest and take stock Leicester trumpeted his hostility to Mary, pushed for her execution and harried the friends of the dead plotters. Catholics now found the fiscal retribution meted out to them began to hurt more than hitherto. If they defaulted on the £20 fine for recusancy the government was now permitted to take two-thirds of their estates. Babington's – from which he had drawn an income stated to have exceeded £1,000 per annum (a modern equivalent might be close to £500,000) – passed to Sir Walter Ralegh, and in a period when the estates of gentlemen usually grew larger, Catholics saw theirs contract, sometimes quite brutally. Taxes on the gentry before 1640 were generally negligible, but the penal levies caused deliberate hardship and a burden that passed down the generations. It was this squeeze on property that was most likely to convince a family (at least its public figures) that the mass was not worth the attendant ruin that could follow. Even so, there were sterner spirits than the Salusburys and Bulkeleys, who had settled to erasing the memory of the errant Thomas whose estate was yet preserved by an old entail. One in whom the spirit of resistance lived on was Sir William Catesby of Lapworth in Warwicksire, with a lineage described as 'ancient, historic and distinguished'. Reconciled to Catholicism by the mission of Persons and Campion, married to a Throckmorton, he suffered imprisonment and the plundering of his wealth. His acceptance of this (whether troubled or indifferent) and the snubbing of his traditional patriotism tilted his son Robert towards armed resistance despite abundant evidence that it would fail. The gunpowder plot used the template of Ballard and Babington, drawing its participants from 'the pupils and converts of the Jesuit mission'.[13] But it was necessarily flawed because it never achieved the critical mass that made its progress unstoppable. The unlucky thirteen main gunpowder plotters had a freight of personal conviction that was quite unmatched among contemporary lay Catholics.

With a foundation of striking presumption they held fast to the view that death in the cause was nothing and ultimately they embraced their end as the prelude to eternal life. A wafer-thin fiction destroyed them. Perhaps it is possible still to find some explanation for this in developments after the execution of Mary and before that of the hapless Earl of Essex in 1601.

A mere six priests had fallen foul of the laws of England and had been executed themselves before the beheading of Mary. But in the following year, 1587, with the country in a state of edgy passivity, waiting for an attack from Spain, the tempo of executions was stepped up and thirty-one died. Also in that year the work of rounding up recusants and valuing their lands was taken from the local authorities and given to operatives of the privy council. Lacking inhibitions based on personal familiarity they went about their business with an unyielding vigour; a procedure enhanced by a promise of an 'allowance out of the forfeitures' they should secure, and also by the first chance to purchase from the queen the lease of confiscated lands. The early missionary successes proved to be temporary and collapsed as the war against Spain continued after the Armada crisis into the next decade. There remained a pervasive fear of attack and a national preoccupation with war. The efforts to dissolve lay Catholic allegiance to Elizabeth, which were mounted at home and abroad, led to further executions in the 1590s – eighty-eight in all. The estrangement of the majority of the population from the old faith was now certain, and the government's measures to counter the vituperation of Father Persons and the pro-Spanish party abroad were accepted. 'Policy and ideology converged in England's national energies, which were largely directed to defensive as opposed to aggressive or interventionist ends.' Not everyone favoured the brisk efforts of Essex in his leadership of the Cadiz expedition (1596) and the Islands voyage (1597). As Thomas Wilson noted in *The State of England, Ann. Dom. 1600*, the 'common soldiers that are sent out of the realm be of the basest and most inexperienced, the best being reserved to defend from invasion.' But laws to prohibit could also entice, and in court circles Catholicism had a fluttering fitful glamour as the late cult of Eliza took on a rather desperate air. The sort of scepticism about Rome that finds voice in Marlowe's spiritual drama *Dr Faustus*, could yet open the way to a nostalgic conversion.

There were tensions, too, within the upper levels of government, involving the tugging of policy by factions. Lord Burghley, ageing and sometimes infirm, came increasingly to rely on the administrative skills of his younger son Sir Robert Cecil. They shared not only the primary tasks of office as ministers, but also an identical dislike of minorities, the improvident and dissident. In what seems like a deliberate contrast there was Essex who benignly gave such provocative elements neglected space, jobs and support whenever he identified an opportunity – and if it ruffled the Cecilians that was a pleasurable bonus. As the heir of his stepfather Leicester (d. 1588), the young earl had puritan support as well, and he married Walsingham's daughter, the widow of the great Protestant hero Sir Philip Sidney. But among Essex's closest friends were the dashing Earl of Southampton, an unsteady Catholic, and Sir Oliver Manners, who had turned back to the old faith. The convert cast of mind found expression in the works of Henry Constable, who had been at St John's College, Cambridge, just before Robert Cecil, and had

Catholic kinsfolk, including priests and nuns from the large Babthorpe family; the conversion of Constable himself seems to have taken place in 1591.[14] A letter that he wrote to Essex in October 1595 is revealing, for in it he declared that 'he was more affectionate to him than to any' and although there was a gap between them on religious matters, the fact that this had forced him to depend on others had been against his will. He then claimed – as many of his co-religionists would have done – that although passionately devoted to Catholicism, he did not wish its restoration in England, nor the servitude of his country to a foreign tyranny, and that he had on several occasions dissuaded some of his Catholic countrymen from violence 'and such as be in authority in the church from approving of them'.

Writing on the same day to Anthony Bacon who had returned to England from a lengthy (and not untroubled) sojourn in France to take control of Essex's intelligence operations, Constable wrote: 'An honest man may be a Catholic and no fool.' Some time later the poet wrote again to Essex in terms that suggest the growth of a friendly understanding between them. He renewed his protests of lawful affection for his country and said that he had written to Rome to dissuade the Pope from believing that English Catholics actually favoured Spanish designs against Elizabeth who had just passed her 'climacteric' of sixty-three years (a number loaded with significance for Elizabethans). Sir Robert Cecil and Essex were both advised of Constable's movements and apparent intentions, and on 12 September 1598 Sir Thomas Edmondes wrote to the former from Paris that there was a project afoot to send Constable to Scotland to encourage James VI to allow Catholics there 'a toleration of Religion', and to assure him of the devoted support of English Catholics. In March of the following year George Nicholson reported to Cecil from Edinburgh that Constable had arrived from France, and the Laird of Boniton, another Catholic, had travelled with him. Yet several days after, Roger Aston informed Cecil that James had refused Constable an audience; the king rejected the notion of toleration. However, despite a summons before the Lords of Sessions, by August of that year Constable and Boniton were indeed negotiating on behalf of the Pope with the king. The object, cited in a despatch from the London ambassador of France to Henri IV, was to win liberty of conscience for Catholics 'et declarer la guerre à la Royne d'Angleterre, lui offrant pour cest affect grand denier et l'assistance de tous les Princes catholiques de la Chrestienté et d'ung grand nombre de Catholiques de ce royaume.'[15]

The mission was not a success and there was some disbelief in political circles in London, rather more closely informed than the French ambassador after long years of monarch watching, that James had ever seriously considered cutting 'the grass under Her Majesty's feet'. When Henry Constable returned to Antwerp from Scotland, Thomas Phelippes, sometime spy coordinator and code-breaker to Walsingham, received a letter from his agent in Brussels who used the alias John Petit. He reported Constable now keeping company with a priest named Tempest and the Earl of Westmorland. One day when out walking they met a young English lad who worked for an exiled printer (probably the gifted and indefatigable Richard Verstegen), 'and asked him what books are printing against the King of Scotland's title; he said he knew of none.' Constable's view of James had evidently shifted and he thought now that the king relied on 'no party in

Henri IV of France was no role model for James I since he had deserted the Huguenots for Catholicism, and enfuriated many on both sides of the sectarian divide

England but the Puritans, and will enter with that pretence, and before the tree falls, if he can find opportunity.'

Evidently Constable was far from elated by his contacts with James, retreating from his former position of supporting him and making some rather disparaging comments. Petit again to Thomas Phelippes (alias Peter Halins): 'he has been as backward for the King of Scots as he was forward before; he speaks of him as little better than an atheist, of no courage nor judgment, and says he and his intend to make havoc of England when the day comes.' Even so, with no other significant candidate to succeed the childless Elizabeth remotely acceptable to his countrymen Constable thought to persevere with James, and he may have been the author of a book the king received that denounced the notorious *Conference about the Next Succession to the Crown of England*, which appeared earlier in the decade with the alias R. Doleman for its author. This name was actually a cover for a collaboration between its essential author, Richard Verstegen, and its reviser Father Persons, a master of style in English and Latin. A text which Constable along with many others ascribed solely to him, it had repercussions in the succession debate that the stiff old queen tried to ward off. It was circulated on the continent late in the autumn of 1593, and a larger edition was printed in 1594 in Antwerp with a dedication to Essex. Optimism or an exile's impertinence?

Arguments for a Spanish successor to the English throne had circulated since 1571, when a secretary to Thomas Percy, 7th Earl of Northumberland, wrote them down. Once married, Archduchess–Infanta Isabella became deeply sceptical of such a notion

The book's first purpose was to discredit the principle of legitimism 'in favour of a contractual theory of sovereignty', and then secondly to rubbish the claims of all save one person. James might briefly have hoped that the emotion generated by the execution of his mother would rally her Catholic supporters to his side. However, Verstegen and others in exile wanted a genuinely Catholic candidate to oust all others. Their book 'brought together arguments for a Spanish successor which had been circulating since 1571'.[16] Their choice was the Infanta Isabella, daughter of Philip II, based on what we might regard as a rather strained ancestral argument, but she was a princess whose faith was unimpeachable. As far as James was concerned it was the most dangerous book of its time. More moderate Catholics looked to Lady Arabella Stuart, cousin of James, since she had been born in England and he had not. After the publication of Doleman her name was regularly noted high on the list of claimants, and there was also talk of her being married to Ranuccio Farnese, one of the sons of the Duke of Parma. Commentators and many politicians did take Doleman very seriously too, and the book naturally became the prized handbook of the Spanish party. James was advised that there was an urgent need for a Protestant pro-Stuart counter to this insidious text, and he was urged as well to woo the common lawyers in England. This was because they were rich and influential in government and held the key to his legal status. Men trained in law had been solid servants of the queen and they had to be convinced of his right to be considered native born, and of a chiming of interests.

The sustained and sometimes furious bickering of the 'Spanish' and 'Scottish' factions among the exiled Catholics reached its climax during the years 1596–1601. Each grouping was then busy denouncing the other to the Pope, the archduke and the King of Spain. The whole thing became merged in the deeper-seated strife between Jesuits and seculars which found expression in 1598 in the domestic exchanges known as the Archpriest controversy. Persons and those who thought as he did, infuriated the secular clergy who regarded them contemptuously as a 'Hispanicized faction', and who credited them as being the real cause of the harsh laws against Catholics in general. As for Henry Constable, he was evidently a stalwart in the greater diplomatic tug-of-war and gave it his own particular thrust. He had spent some time in Rome before moving to live in Paris as a pensioner of the Duchess of Vendôme, sister of Henri IV.[17] He continued to write to the Pope and Cardinal Baronio, making proposals for the conversion of England by means of France. In his estimation it was possible because Henri IV had himself made the leap from Huguenot to Catholic for reasons of state. Constable's notion had led to discussions between the cardinal and Persons, but the scorn of the English Jesuit for its lack of a practical basis was enough to convince Baronio that it was flawed. The prelate told Constable that the Pope would not consider the matter.

The Englishman was phlegmatic about this and his views did find favour with certain other English exiles in Flanders. In Paris, too, men of influence chose to regard it with interest and d'Epernon and de Sancy convinced among others the papal nuncio in France. For his part Constable had contacted Dr Stapleton of Louvain; Dr Barrett, then rector of the Douai seminary and Dr William Gifford,

Rapacious, cruel and clever, the Duke d'Epernon far out-classed all English conspirators. He was never caught and may have helped to arrange the murder of Henri IV in 1610

Dean of St Peter's in Lille, who had a somewhat spotted career and was to be paid by the government agent Charles Paget for supplying the English government with information after the gunpowder plot. This friendly contact was already known to Persons, as was Gifford's continued correspondence with the French ambassador in Rome. The Jesuit took the understanding that a scheme was evolving for England to be brought into the French sphere of influence – Antonio Perez, exiled from Spain on charges of treason, had already represented Henri IV to Essex, who too had many Scottish contacts and was greatly esteemed by James. So, through the good offices of Henri there were to be negotiations leading to the granting of qualified religious liberty even during Elizabeth's declining years. On her death the understanding would be that the same religious space and flexibility would continue under the benign rule of James. Persons understood that James had begun already to edge his nobles to a wary agreement and had appointed the Archbishop of Glasgow as his ambassador to France. Further, that promoters of the effort already had their agents in England about Essex and other accessible members of the privy council. Lord Dacre was in Paris with the archbishop and Persons expected him to travel to Scotland for talks with James. As for Constable – he was to be sent to Rome again.

The Spanish ambassador to the papal court, the Duke of Sessia, forwarded news of all this diplomatic activity to his government. On 1 February 1601 the Spanish Council of State reported to Philip III that Constable – named as a great confidant of James – had indeed arrived in Rome, with (it was believed) the consent of the king.[18] The Pope had meanwhile been regaled with the delicious fable that James might be converted to his mother's faith, and even more grandly that if the papacy and Spain joined forces to secure the English succession, then both England and Scotland might at last return to the old faith. This chimed with the strong view of the Jesuits that in monarchical Europe 'it was absolutely essential to capture the sovereign'. Persons stated this line forthrightly in his vast correspondence, even in a letter to the Earl of Angus in January 1600: 'the happiest day that could ever shine to me in this life, were to see both our Realms united together under one Catholic governor.' Angus and James both fathomed the deeper meaning; no conversion, no succession was the implication. Persons at this time was prepared to allow the view that Constable might be sent to sound out James, but the Pope now retreated from giving his consent. He was more concerned that Philip III should quickly opt for whom he wished to succeed Elizabeth, and the Council of State approved of the papal refusal to give a brief to Constable because they feared that James's Protestantism was fixed. Was it possible that the poet-envoy just might be gulled with feigned protestations of conversion in order that James should have the Pope in his pocket?

Clement VIII resisted being an instrument for the policy of the Jesuits and the Spanish monarchy. His settlement of the Archpriest controversy in England had led him to rebuke the former for intemperance, and as the pontiff who had absolved Henri IV he was anxious to find a candidate for the English throne who would be acceptable to France as well as Spain and the English Catholic laity. Lady Arabella Stuart had been considered, but given the delicacy of the situation with her it was still easier to negotiate with James. In 1602 Clement VIII made

A man of peace like James I, Philip III also recoiled from his subjects, frittered away vast sums, and relied on favourites to rule as he became increasingly indolent

him a firm offer of support on condition that Prince Henry was raised as a Catholic. Other less elevated men than the Pope had also to assess their positions in the fading light of the last Tudor. One such was Hugh Owen, the renegade Welsh spy master for the archdukes and Spain, who had had his pension renewed by Philip III in 1601 because the king looked to him to nurture the Spanish cause in England. Not the easiest task, especially since the Infanta Isabella – now married to Archduke Albrecht and so co-ruler of the Spanish Netherlands – was herself highly sceptical of any such proposition. Owen in secret reviewed the matter again, taking account of papal preferences, the attitude of the secular priests in England, as well as the majority of the laity. Towards the end of 1602 he received a clandestine visit from his brother Robert, a canon in the French church, and sent by the French government on a brief to pull together measures on the succession. Their exchanges on the political shape of things-to-come were soon marginalized by the long anticipated death of Elizabeth in March 1603, at which point, since she left no heir and no formally designated successor, any Catholic effort to establish a regime friendly to Catholics (if not Catholic) could not be treason. But it was James VI who became king, being better prepared than anyone else, aided by Sir Robert Cecil and the privy council. The country willed it although some well-placed individuals showed no great enthusiasm, and the intervention of the Earl of Northumberland in his approach to the council, many retainers in tow, certainly upset Cecil and those who stood beside him. This success for James was achieved without any foreign aid and more crucially 'without the need for any active help from his Catholic supporters at home'. It swamped any prospect of real change for them. Blood royal carried the Crown and the day.

It was to be expected that the response of the exiles would not be unanimous; no chorus of approval or disapprobation. Dr Gifford, who had helped to spread the hope of converting James and so offended the pro-Spanish cluster, conveyed to the rapturous king a friendly message from the papal nuncio in Brussels. Hugh Owen later took the view that if Gifford had not persuaded Clement VIII of this supposed impending conversion then the accession would have been a much more disorderly business. Father Henry Garnet, soon to become a prominent figure in the gunpowder conspiracy, wrote to Persons while James was travelling from Edinburgh to London, and was quite buoyant about the prospects for the new regime. His hope that no foreign power would intervene was duly fulfilled. In the seminaries where Persons had many admirers and supporters, Douai and Rome, there was a pause for reflection and for the time being rueful acceptance of the new situation. At Douai the college diary made no comment, although Dr John Worthington who was in charge there was a devoted follower of Persons. The latter had taken on the administration of the English College in Rome five years before the accession of James which was publicly celebrated by a mass on Trinity Sunday. Privately Persons was acutely sceptical about the king in his two realms. In July 1603 in a letter to Garnet he regretted that lack of unified purpose had prevented Catholics from imposing definite terms, but there was some pleasurable relief in the death at last of a hated queen. His comment several months before had been that 'the doubt conceived of the king's religion has cast much water into the wine'.[19] As for Clement VIII, he still hoped that James or Prince Henry would be reconciled, and this was perhaps allowable while he waited for a reply to his offer. The response from James was drafted in October 1602, but the messenger fell ill so that it reached Paris months later for forwarding to Rome. In it James rejected the proposed course, and although his tone was mild no concessions were trailed as they had been previously. Prince Henry was not going to be educated as a Catholic, even if his mother, Queen Anne, was retreating from her childhood Lutheranism.

TWO

Plotters in Exile

It was a striking coincidence not lost upon his contemporaries that James VI of Scotland succeeded Elizabeth on what was then New Year's Eve, 24 March 1603, thus restoring the Golden Age as they imagined with the new year. But the character, pronouncements and publications of his reign beyond the sometimes turbulent border did not disarm or even greatly encourage English Catholic exiles. Their judgments of him varied and the conspiratorially inclined could not be easily persuaded that he would make a principled and generous response to their hurts. The deformities of spirit remained, though after 1598, when the Edict of Nantes in France seemed to show that toleration was a benign option for countries with profound religious divisions, some discerned a faint light of hope. This did not touch James, whose real attitude towards Catholicism derived from the same roots as his views on Puritanism – a hostility that was much more political than religious.[1] He hated toleration and this matched the view of the man who emerged as his chief minister – Sir Robert Cecil. No doubt sensitive adjudication between Catholics and James was possible, but Cecil was not the man to do it, and the notion of armed resistance by the religious minority had an allure for some before 1605. A soldier in exile like Sir William Stanley, whose name was synonymous in England with treachery, certainly preferred bullets to compromise. For years he had sought 'to promote his own standing and prestige in the Spanish military service by playing a prominent part in an invasion to some part of the British Isles'.

With their royal blood, the Stanleys had inevitably a somewhat bumpy relationship with Elizabeth, especially after the plot in 1570 led by Sir Thomas and Sir Edward Stanley, to free Mary, Queen of Scots from Chatsworth and take her to the Isle of Man. A cousin of the Earl of Derby, William Stanley (b. 1548) had earned a brilliant reputation as a soldier, first serving with the Duke of Alva in the Netherlands, and then in Ireland under the Deputy, Lord Grey, being knighted in September 1579. Stanley won further acclaim for his martial acumen during the first part of the fitful campaign of the Earl of Leicester to assist the Dutch rebels against Spain. From late 1585–6 Stanley organized a levy in Ireland that sent over a thousand troops to assist, and he fought in the Zutphen engagement that became infamous for the wound taken by Sir Philip Sidney which led to an abominable lingering death. By December 1586, while Elizabeth deliberated over Stanley's promotion to Viceroy of Ireland, he was frantically drawing attention to his situation and that of his men in the Low Countries. On

After his bizarre childhood it is not surprising James I became an opinionated and eccentric ruler of England

the 26th of that month he wrote to Walsingham: 'I am at his time driven to lay all my apparell to pawn in the Lombard, for money to pay for meat and drink . . . Were it not in respect of my duty to her Majesty I could as well run my head into a stone wall as endure it.' The captains with him were subsisting on bread and cheese, while the ordinary soldiers were reduced to half a pound of cheese a day, unrelieved by bread or even an onion. This meant that many became sick and Stanley had no money to help. 'We have not received a month's pay since our coming into these countries, which is now almost six months.'[2]

Driven to exasperated revolt by his immediate situation, which did not seem likely to improve, Stanley made the remarkable decision to surrender the town of Deventer to the Spanish in January 1587. This was what we might call a gut decision, but ironically it made no difference as agents and spies almost gleefully reported to London. About a year after the surrender Sir Ralph Sadler noted the atrocious condition of the regiment under Spanish control, forced to winter in the field and subsist on dry acorns. One of Stanley's Irish captains, Oliver Eustace, upbraided him for this, saying that Stanley had brought them to a parlous situation and was duty bound to relieve their suffering. In the meantime, Stanley was applauded by the Jesuits and finely defended in print by Dr William Allen. As for the beneficiary of the defection – Philip II – he was reported to have commented rather grudgingly that he liked the act of handing over the town but not the traitor. Stanley was excluded from the Armada preparations against England, and this went on for years afterwards; the Spanish attitude had a stubborn hold and being unable to shift it Stanley set much greater store by the efforts of the English Catholic exiles, and the regiment became identified with these. It may have been called the 'English regiment', but it was actually a multi-national mercenary force of some 700 Irish, English, Welsh, Scots, Italians, Burgundians and later, Walloons. The Spanish sources were remarkably clear in saying 626 soldiers and 90 officers (mostly English) defected to them, and were later joined by Captain Sir Rowland Yorke's group and some 200 Catholic refugee gentlemen. But very soon this figure of some 1,200 officers and men had plummeted, and by 1589 it was in danger of being disbanded. Morale was not assisted by the self-serving efforts of one of Stanley's own officers who saw a chance to redirect his rickety career as a soldier and double agent.

The man was Jacomo di Franceschi, more often known by his contemporaries as Captain Jacques. According to a report in the papers of Sir Ralph Sadler, this violent and subversive soldier was born in Antwerp of Italian parents, but had been brought up in England since early childhood.[3] There is a reference to him in the confession of Anthony Babington where he says he met Franceschi some three years before in France and he calls him a soldier of Ireland. Certainly Franceschi had been a subordinate of Sir John Perrot in Ulster, and simultaneously he seems to have acted as an intelligencer for Sir Christopher Hatton in London. By 1585 Franceschi was lieutenant to Stanley, but late in the year he was mixing freely with the Babington conspirators in London whose activities were known to Stanley and the privy council, so that Walsingham and his agents knew every move of the plotters and probably the boast of Franceschi to Edward Windsor that he would raise an insurrection in Ireland whence he had lately returned. While there Franceschi received a letter from Stanley, now in the Low Countries with his Irish Kernes, inviting him to join him, and this may add a little weight to the suggestion that Stanley's betrayal of Deventer was less occasioned by suffering than premeditated treachery. Franceschi did not immediately join him and when Stanley had done his best to head off the fast-approaching execution of Mary, Queen of Scots, the privy council in London wrote to the Lord Deputy in Ireland to keep a watchful eye on all Stanley's secret friends and dependants. In particular they marked out Franceschi for being 'a stranger ill-affected in religion' and for his contacts with the Babington conspirators. Following this Franceschi seems to have spent some time in the Fleet prison, while maintaining a correspondence with a young Irishman of noble birth, Florence MacCarthy. The two fought together in Munster against Desmond, and it seems likely that 'servants and retainers' of MacCarthy had gone as a group with Stanley. When the young man aspired to make a grand marriage alliance (which took place in 1588) he was encouraged by Franceschi.[4] The President of Munster suggested to London that Franceschi's complicity in this thoroughly misliked nuptial should be 'boulted' out of him. As it happened, MacCarthy was arrested and sent to the Tower, while at length Franceschi was freed to go to the Low Countries in 1589 where on becoming lieutenant-colonel of Stanley's declining regiment he launched very promptly into mischief. According to the imprisoned Catholic informer Anthony Copley, 'Jacques, I supposed wisheth himself in Ireland again, seeing how much his hope of advancement in Flanders . . . is coming to nothing.' By August 1590 Franceschi was working up an elaborate plan to disperse the regiment with Sir Thomas Morgan, commander of the English forces in the Low Countries fighting for the Dutch. With secret assistance from Franceschi, Morgan was to take over the fort of Ordam, where Stanley's regiment was stationed. The plan folded because Morgan went down with a fever and Stanley removed to another place.[5] It was, incidentally, a plan approved by Elizabeth on the advice of Burghley, who after the death of Walsingham in April 1590 took on the direction of secret agents in the Low Countries. Probably he was persuaded to give responsibilities to Franceschi by Sir Christopher Hatton who had long favoured him with 'courtesies which for ever would have tied a thankful mind'.

There was now a bitter rift between Stanley and Franceschi, and while the former planned an invasion of Alderney in the Channel Islands for 1591, the latter waylaid English Catholic refugees and spun out talk of assassinating Elizabeth. One who met him in Antwerp in 1592 wrote: 'One day a Mr Jacques came to dinner, whom I never saw before that time. He was attired in black satin, with a man attending on him. He uttered these, or the like words, at the table: "By God, they say in England I would have killed the Queen, but, by God, belie me." What he was I am not able to say; he was slender and reasonably tall of stature, and had a black beard; and had been, as he said, a follower of the deceased Lord Chancellor' (Hatton). Rifts in Stanley's regiment, which naturally drifted towards being the armed extension of the English Catholic exiles, rather than an active service unit of the Spanish armies in Flanders, stemmed for the most part from want of money and the rivalry for Spanish and papal funds. Not having secure financial resources for all, the perceived urgent work was doubly tormenting because not only were the Spanish haphazard in allocations, but the wealth and estates left behind in England benefited their enemies. The letters of the exiles are crammed with references to privation and political inconsequence. They could freeze in winter and starve at any time, although 1587–9 was particularly terrible because of a famine there. If the Baltic grain ships and Spanish treasure fleets did not deliver then their situation became parlous. So an old campaigner like Sir Thomas Markenfeld, who lived in a Brussels tenement, was found dead of starvation during the summer of 1592 'lying on the bare floor of his chamber, no creature being present at his death'.[6]

The hopeless conjunction of exile and acute distress in poverty could lead men into wild schemes. Perhaps coiners and counterfeiters could do something to assist. Along the loop of this illegal activity which worried the privy council in London, we find a sometime spy and playwright, Christopher Marlowe, in Flushing at the beginning of 1592 with a goldsmith and a former Catholic priest who should have been able to link them up with the exiles. I believe Marlowe and company were sent there on a mission by Burghley, and if we step back a little we may see why. In 1589 Marlowe and his friend the poet Thomas Watson had spent some time in Newgate prison after an affray in which a man died. They had been detained with one John Poole, a Catholic with family connections to the Stanleys. By marriage to Mary Stanley he had become brother-in-law to Sir William whom he defended at length when drawn out by another government spy; Poole was also well informed on the matter of counterfeiting and who was to know if Sir William had benefited from this as he grumpily reiterated that he had been defrauded by Ralegh. As Stanley planned his Alderney venture, the Earl of Essex was not very far away from there campaigning in Normandy to assist Henri of Navarre in his struggle against the Catholic league led by the Duc de Mayenne. With Essex went a clutch of Catholic maverick soldiers and freebooters who seized the opportunity to join him and so quit the country unhindered. And once abroad they deserted to Stanley who was then in action near Nijmegen. Among those who did this was the Welsh Catholic Richard Williams, the ringleader of the raid on Winchester cathedral which had cost the Church dear, and once there Williams was quickly within the orbit of the dangerous Captain Jacques with whom he was reportedly 'very great'.[7]

The burglary had been carried out in company with Captains Dyer and Duffield, as well as Edward Bushell, grandson of a Throckmorton, his mother a Winter and his cousins Sheldons, Treshams and Catesbys. At this time Bushell was retainer in the household of Ferdinando Stanley, Lord Strange, cousin of Sir William Stanley, who had made the case to Robert Persons for his relative to be regarded as a suitable pretender to the English crown. According to testimony given later by Henry Young to the government, Williams claimed they had seized plate and money amounting to some £1,800 – the plate being turned into coin. This was necessarily a substantial effort that drew in 'divers gentlemen that saw the plate coined into money and had shares therein'. Somewhat improbably all this was undertaken in the chamber at Gray's Inn of Sir Griffin Markham, who 'belonged to the raffish section of Court converts'.[8] Like so many of these

ill-directed swordsmen he spent his time 'gaming, haunting the lords of opposition and adventuring in foreign wars'. A cousin of Babington and Richard Williams, it became hard to exclude Markham from conspiracy. As for Dyer and Duffield – both fit the latter description of Markham. There was a Captain Robert Dyer in Stanley's regiment, and early in 1592 Henry Duffield was reported to Burghley as 'a discontented man, and bitter in invectives against the State'. It was said that Duffield was plotting a raid on the queen's fleet at Chatham.

The highly successful raid on the queen's church at Winchester meanwhile suggested another get-rich-quick opportunity to Williams and his gang. He confessed later that they came to London with the equipment they had used on the church ready to stage a raid on Whitehall Palace to seize royal jewels and plate. The haul would likely have been enormous because Elizabeth regularly added to her collection and did not lightly dispose of the choicest items. Whatever the 'engine' was that they used, it made sufficient noise for one of the raiders to panic. When the others declined to stop he caused a commotion and Captain Dyer wanted to kill him on the spot. Instead he wounded him 'very shrewdly' and the victim of the hurt was then carried into St George's Fields where he was ordered to keep silent or they would finish him off and bury him on the spot. Whatever evidence was found of this failed effort there is every reason to suppose that an astonished and mortified government set about secret attempts to trace the emboldened thieves with their cathedral loot. Indeed, for Burghley and his son Robert Cecil who was increasingly engaged in government work at a high level, to have allowed a sum with a modern equivalent of perhaps £900,000 to pass unhindered into the pockets of the queen's sworn enemies would have been an unthinkable dereliction. Their clear duty was to go after it and the culprits because of the potential damage it could do if it reached the English Catholic exiles – and how else did Captain Jacques find the money for his black satin suit and his servant?

One Irishman whom Burghley and his son regarded with increasing irritation and some justified suspicion was Michael Moody.[9] The ex-jailbird, who had spent some time in the Tower for planning to kill Elizabeth by putting gunpowder under her bed, was now a spy working for all sides in the Low Countries 'resolute to dispatch any enterprise for money'. Late in 1591 he was warned not to visit Flushing so often, evidently because the Cecils wanted some working space for Marlowe, Gilbert the goldsmith and Baines, sometime priest and spy. My view is that they were sent to try to trace the Winchester haul in its latest form, and to spook the exiled plotters who were regrouping for another attempt on Elizabeth's life. Gifford Gilbert remains something of an unknown quantity in the equation, but we can be sure he was selected for a purpose; who better to spot clipping or counterfeiting? Or if the exiles required assistance in converting the rest of their haul into coin he was available, although in England such activity was equated with treason – which put him on an equal footing with the exiles. Evidently Gilbert made some coins, English currency and a Dutch shilling in pewter, probably with a silver wash, that got into circulation, and almost immediately these modest items sent Baines (late in 1591 or early in 1592) on a little mission to betray the effort to the English governor of Flushing, Sir Robert Sidney, younger brother of the late courtier–soldier. The ex-seminarian betrayed a man who had once famously derided the Catholic Church in his play *Dr Faustus*, and he did it precipitately in order to protect possible Catholic contacts among the exiles. He cloaked his intention rather neatly by saying that Marlowe was preparing to go over 'to the enemy or to Rome' – a fine catch-all phrase that would commit Sidney to do something. So the accused were indeed arrested and kept under English restraint, rather than handed over to the town's officials, before being interrogated. Marlowe then made a simple counter-accusation against Baines (he had to say something), and easily managed to confuse Sidney who always felt somewhat adrift in the world of spies and counter-spies. Marlowe's intention not to blow his own cover is evident from his suppression of the name of his employer (Burghley; a fact that Baines had evidently guessed), and by his citing as references the names of Lord Strange and the Earl of Northumberland. Any spy in Sidney's household for the exiles would have been excited to hear this since it signalled as Marlowe intended, where his sympathies lay, as Sir William was keenly supporting his kinsman's claim to the English throne. The testimony of Baines lacked specificity, but it suggests now that Marlowe had indeed made contacts with the Catholic exiles before the mission was aborted. The playwright, Gilbert and one Evan Flud (a Henry Flud and a John Flud were respectively captain and lieutenant in Stanley's regiment), were sent back to England under arrest, and Marlowe was interviewed by Burghley at the end of January 1592. I doubt if the old Lord Treasurer gave his agent very much of a welcome, though just before Marlowe's sudden death in May 1593 he may have been considering using him again. It was not until immediately after this tragic event that Sir William Stanley's plot to kill Elizabeth was thwarted, and it was then nipped so closely that it has not even acquired a name for identification.

But the exiles were rarely deflected for long from preparing for treason, and so it was with Richard Williams and Edmund Yorke, nephew of Captain Rowland Yorke, whose company of lancers had been disbanded in 1588 after the failure of the Armada. In 1594 Williams and Yorke were sent by Father William Holt and the indefatigable Stanley to do what all other plotters had failed to do. To secure admittance to England both men intended to renounce publicly their service with the enemy, but they had not reckoned on their companion, Henry Young, turning queen's evidence the moment they were taken. He had himself been well known to Marlowe, and once Williams and Yorke were in custody they too made confessions that almost did for Edward Bushell.[10] His employer, Lord Strange, so wistfully regarded by the exiles, had spurned all efforts to woo him into treachery and he now became the Earl of Derby. But in April, swiftly and shockingly, he died, so that many suspected either witchcraft, or poisoning before the Williams/Yorke treason was fully prepared. The confession made by Williams implicated Bushell's cousin, the wealthy Worcestershire landowner Ralph Sheldon, who proved adept at skirting the loaded question – such as, did he harbour Catholic priests in his house? Since he had not lost Elizabeth's favour Sheldon emerged from this uncomfortable period. As for Bushell, he seems to have served the widowed Lady Derby for a time (rather than the new earl), before shifting to Essex's household where eventually he became a gentleman-usher. No

Fawkes, the mercenary soldier, here looks as if he has an easy nonchalance

wonder the Essex revolt in 1601 had a curious slant given to it by the minority of disaffected religious malcontents who took part, men for whom a whiff of treason was as addictive as tobacco. As for the gunpowder plot – it was their last sensational effort, coloured by all that had gone before over some twenty years.

For Ned Bushell insurrection seems to have been a gentleman's diversion, an adult's luxury of dangerous play that kept him in England. He held back from the sale of his property. Not so Guy Fawkes, whose name today is inextricably part of the gunpowder plot and is celebrated by children of all ages with dangerous play. Fawkes sold his modest inheritance, his mother Edith having remarried, before leaving for a prolonged exile and a necessarily somewhat precarious mercenary existence in the Spanish service, after enlisting in 1593. Born in April 1570 he was the son of Edward Fawkes, proctor and advocate of the Consistory Court at York according to one source, although he may have followed his own father into the post of Registrar of the Exchequer Court of the Archbishop. Initially stationed in France, Guy had moved (probably after 1596) to Stanley's regiment which had itself been through a number of vicissitudes. No sooner had the sceptical Philip II died in 1598 of a portmanteau of diseases, than Stanley, Fawkes and Thomas Winter (of whom more later) tried to win the approval of Philip III for a revival of a Stanley scheme for the invasion of England. In brief, it required the Spanish to seize control of Milford Haven so that their fleet commanded the passage to Ireland which would also serve as a useful base. Spanish troops would march from Llandovery to Builth and Brecon before dividing into Herefordshire, Warwickshire, Staffordshire and Worcestershire – counties most populated with Catholic gentry. Stanley, Owen, Father Holt and Richard Stanihurst (who had once thought to procure the assassination of Antonio Perez by one of Stanley's Irish captains, Oliver Eustace), drew up a report on the military resources of the exiles 'in the event that Your Majesty has the intention of proceeding further in the claiming of the realm of England and Ireland for the Infanta'. The report also put the case for better pay and more recruits.

Fawkes was a champion of the Jesuits, as was Hugh Owen, who also proved to be a dedicated adversary of two generations of Elizabethan spy masters. He tangled with Walsingham and Burghley, and then with Robert Cecil who developed a profound antipathy towards him. Owen came from a Welsh gentry family, one of the sons of Owen ap Gruffydd of Plas Du, near Pwllheli, and his wife Margaret, daughter of Fulke Salusbury of Llanwrst.[11] Hugh and his brother Robert (who also figures sporadically in the annals of the emigrés) were probably educated in the household of Henry Fitzalan, Earl of Arundel, who became a leading supporter of Mary, Queen of Scots. In his wake was Hugh Owen, who found himself working with his master in the Ridolfi plot. Indeed, he was given the essential task of arranging relays of horses for her and providing an escort abroad. By October 1571 Burghley had warrants out for Owen's arrest and after a

One of the foreign claimants to the English throne, the Duke of Parma had a brilliant career as a professional soldier serving Spain. His son was for a time thought of as a possible husband for Lady Arabella Stuart, cousin of King James

period of sanctuary with various sympathizers in north-west Shropshire he fled abroad permanently. His brother Robert had already gone before him, entering the college of Douai and paying his own expenses. Hugh, however, had no inclination to join the priesthood and certainly never became a Jesuit, such as was once erroneously suggested by a great historian. Nor for that matter did he become a professional soldier as Fawkes would, although in 1572 Owen was in Spain before quitting Madrid to return to the Spanish Netherlands. With him he took the promise of a pension – it proved hard to convert into actual coins – and the possibility of employment as a field messenger to be available wherever there was fighting. It was on one of these errands that he and Persons were very nearly captured by English soldiers issuing from Mechlin. By this time (in the 1580s) Owen was readily favoured by the leading general of the Spanish in the field, Alessandro Farnese, Duke of Parma. So it was in the period 1584–6 that Persons, Cardinal Allen and Owen formed the trio to whom Philip II assigned the dealings with Parma over the very last attempt to rescue Mary, Queen of Scots. As we have noted, the so-called Babington plot led not only to the destruction of Babington and his confederates, but ultimately to the execution of Mary, and an end to her self-serving presence in England at last.

Hugh Owen's lodgings *à l'image S. Michel* in the Brussels cheese market (a spot that must have been rather repugnant to Stanley) became the headquarters of the counter-espionage efforts servicing successive archdukes.[12] Parma's successors as governors of the Spanish Netherlands, Ernst and Albrecht (Albert – captain general as well of the army), who married the Infanta Isabella, also came to regard the Welshman as indispensable; 'ruling all courses for England' was the view of the time. About him was a cabal of like-minded men including William Myddleton, another Welshman, who had left behind his business in London to move to Flanders; Richard Verstegen, antiquary and printer who had quit England to go back to the place of his forebears, and had a house of his own that became (much to the irritation of Persons) a comfortable meeting-place and a central mailing address; Charles Bailly (Bayley), tortured for involvement in the Ridolfi plot; and more remotely Robert Owen, who liaised with English Catholic exiles over the border in France. The letters between the two Owen brothers (tricked out with bits of Welsh for close secrets) were addressed to Dr John Davison, professor of laws, whose rooms at Cambrai College, Paris, made another convenient postal bureau. He acted as the forwarding agent for items despatched from England, France, Spain, Flanders and Rome. He stood too as banker for the exiles when necessary. On one occasion he lent £50 to Father John Gerard when the Jesuit visited him in company with Everard Digby who was to be lured into the gunpowder plot in its last days. Digby was wealthy enough even then to be regarded as a prime catch by Robert Catesby.

THREE

The Failed Plots

There was an ephemeral and clumsy part-rehearsal for the gunpowder plot a full two years before that strange and lurid episode. The Bye plot (or 'Surprise' treason) had, of course, different leaders and a different locale. The intention was to capture James on Midsummer night 1603, in order to force from him certain concessions – notably the religious toleration that he found so poisonous a concept. William Watson and William Clarke were two secular priests, both fiercely anti–Jesuit. Watson had been sent into Scotland to visit James on behalf of English Catholics before the death of Elizabeth, a journey paid for by Sir Griffin Markham, and later he indignantly represented that James had then given them (through Watson) a most solemn promise of toleration. Now he had achieved his goal of the throne it was said he had jettisoned such notions, a proceeding that enraged the priests so that Watson threw himself into conspiracy, assuring all who listened that seizing the king was lawful as he was not yet crowned. Those approached were asked to take an oath of secrecy which ended: 'this oath is voluntarily taken by me in simple and plain terms, without all equivocation and deceit, and religiously to be kept, I attest, so help me God and holy doom.' The curiosity of this is that the oath itself was equivocal, as it has recently been pointed out. It bound the swearer 'not to reveal anything . . . without advice and consent of twelve of the chief thereof', but since there were never more than a handful of chief contrivers as Watson admitted, the terms of the oath were bogus. Counting the gunpowder plotters also presents a problem, but it is generally accounted to be Robert Catesby and twelve others.

The two priests travelled hither and thither amongst Catholic county families, calling upon them to come forward in the name of their religion and in defence of their property. Watson's economy with the truth was further instanced by Anthony Copley, one of his accomplices, when under examination in July 1603. In order to draw in 'associates of the better sort' and those who were nervous of involvement, the oath presenters intimated that the episode was to be no more than a supplication to James 'for an assuage of our grievance'. Then having taken the oath the more active and boldest individuals were to be told of the deep plan to seize James. If there was an agent provocateur nudging Watson then Copley himself would be a suitable candidate. A volatile man, a hater of Jesuits, he was the brother-in-law of John Gage, whose family were to be found in some numbers at Wormsley, Herefordshire. In the same county Watson's views had an influence on Roger Cadwallader.

Sir Robert Cecil received warnings of the Bye plot from a variety of sources, so having intelligencers at home as well as abroad proved a benefit. The chief justice,

Sir John Popham, also had agents about and one of them encountered a handful of rebels in arms at Tewkesbury.[1] They were 'well appointed with pistols' and according to one of the servants in attendance they were riding to London. He blurted out with a hint of anxiety – 'I pray God we break not our skins before we come back again.' Yet it transpired that they saw no action at all and might have withdrawn to their homes without proper scrutiny but for Popham dining with Bancroft, Bishop of London, on 18 July. From him he learned more names of suspects, although unlike the Essex rebellion no significant leader emerged to take the reins of effort. The new Catholic peers of the reign were very reluctant to risk so much so early, and failing in that section of society. Watson had to cast about for further support, even approaching Thomas, Lord Grey of Wilton, regarded as the leader of the Puritans. He too declined to be involved, but his name was bandied about to convince some would-be conspirators who hesitated at seizing the sovereign, that James was to be taken in order to forestall a Puritan plot! It was Bancroft who named two Herefordshire men – Parry and Vaughan – neither of whom were known to have made any move, just as Lord Grey himself held off. With these two former names in mind Popham recalled now the information he had received from Tewkesbury, and he reasoned now that they had been involved in some treasonable purpose.

Among the hitherto unidentified plotters was John Parry of Poston, the son and heir of the late master of the buckhounds to Elizabeth, James Parry, with

His ill-composed behaviour in the face of royal dislike evidently made Ralegh consider treason in a new light in 1603. The Tower beckoned!

A personal enemy of Lord Cobham and Sir Walter Ralegh, Henry Howard, Earl of Northampton, was almost 'a perfect specimen of cultivated aristocratic villainy'

family connections scattered widely over Herefordshire and Breconshire. John Parry's companions were Richard Croft (closely related to Sir Herbert Croft) and Richard Davies, who lived just outside Poston. Another privy to the plot was John Scudamore of Kentchurch – not seen in Tewkesbury, but linked by confessions made in London and subsequent developments. The fissures in the Catholic community are now highlighted by the fact that the government got confirmation of its suspicions from the archpriest George Blackwell, and from the Jesuits. Blackwell's channel to Cecil, assuring the government of Catholic loyalty, was John Gage, and his kinsman Copley was arrested because his famous timidity would likely have led him to blab. Catholics and government alike were antipathetic towards Puritans and Sir Walter Ralegh found himself in a very exposed position, detested by Watson, who aimed to remove him when James was taken, and regarded as a personal rival by the court Catholic Earl of Northampton and Cecil. The arrest of Ralegh may originally have been intended to widen the government's knowledge of the Bye plotters, including Sir Griffin Markham, once a supporter of Essex and now swamped by debts; George Brooke, brother of Lord Cobham and hence Cecil's brother-in-law, and Anthony Champney. The dry comment of Cecil was that the mere fact of Brooke being involved made him suspicious of Cobham, Ralegh and Henry Percy, Earl of Northumberland. They were all apprehended for involvement in what became known as the Main plot. Such simultaneity does not make the task of the historian any easier. What is certain is that those in power used both to eliminate personal rivals.

The hostility of the Jesuits was seen by Watson as a critical restraint on his supporters in Wales moving on London. He had uneasily anticipated this falling away while in conversation with Copley; and so it proved. Only John Harries of Haverfordwest and a posse of some thirty appeared, and once the government had a line on the conspirators from Herefordshire the project swiftly folded. The sheriff there was soon able to report that John Scudamore had been arrested, his house at Kentchurch searched. When the prisoner reached London he was examined by Sir William Waad and he admitted links to Watson who had been at Kentchurch in mid-July and may have intended to flee to Ireland. That never came about because by the end of the month Watson was under arrest, almost certainly secured by Henry Vaughan of Moccas.[2]

The fumblings of Watson and Clarke (what was he about at this time?) did nothing to enhance the reputation of the Earl of Northumberland. The folding of one plot into another certainly had uncomfortable repercussions for the man whose marriage to Lady Arabella Stuart had once been urged. She was the figurehead in the so-called Main plot and according to one account regicide was to have been a violent preliminary to her succession to the throne. It is true that those named as the Main plotters – Ralegh, Cobham, Brooke, Lord Grey and Markham – were seething with various grievances. For example, Ralegh had lost his post as Captain of the Guard and felt keenly the ignominy of being ejected from old Durham House, his palatial residence on the Thames. He and Cobham had been excluded from the new privy council, and Ralegh certainly resented the enhanced position of Cecil. The first cast of the plotters was to France for funds, but Henri IV would have nothing to do with them. Next they approached

Archduke Albrecht through his London envoy, Charles de Ligne, Comte d'Aremberg. The instruction he received from Brussels was to give a favourable response to the plotters who intended to obtain some 500,000 to 600,000 crowns from the Spanish treasury. This was vital for a maverick like Markham, so much in debt that a warrant was out for his arrest even before the plots. It was Aremberg's aide, La Rensy, who was spotted by government spies in meetings with Cobham, and when asked about these Ralegh denied all knowledge of them to the privy council. Then he stumbled into an error that made him and Cobham vulnerable to pressure from Cecil. Realizing that Cobham had once left Durham House to visit La Rensy and alarmed that this would have been reported, Ralegh sought to mitigate any inference from it by declaring it himself to Cecil, thus contradicting his previous submission to the privy council.[3] This letter had an aggravating effect since it coincided with the confession of George Brooke whose loyalty to the plotters evaporated; there is even the possibility that he was (as it has been claimed) a spy for Cecil. According to Brooke the huge sums of money sought from France and then Spain had been 'to assist and furnish a secret action for the surprise of his Majesty' – a somewhat bland version of the intention to kill James and his immediate family.

Ralegh was sent to the Tower and in a trance of bemused anger and dismay seems to have made a half-hearted attempt at suicide. His trial was delayed, but rather by a combination of the plague, the coronation of James late in July and the presence still in England of Aremberg. With a touching regard for established diplomatic proprieties it was felt his intrigues could not be revealed yet and to expel him was too embarrassing. So the trials were stalled until the ambassador quit the country in October. Then all the Bye plotters were condemned by their own confessions after trial in mid-November. Only Sir Edward Parham was acquitted after pleading that he joined solely to rescue the king if his would-be captors got to him. Cecil's mild intervention on his behalf allowed a rare verdict of not guilty, and so an air of impartiality was given to the proceedings.

The trial of Ralegh was held in Winchester on 17 November; the trials of Cobham and Grey on 25 and 26 November. The town was chosen because James and the court had quit London for Oxford and had finally settled at the Earl of Pembroke's vast Wilton estate. It was there that some of the foreign ambassadors who had come to present greetings from brother rulers finally got to meet James during the time of the trials. In some measure Ralegh's imperturbability had returned; a verdict against him was not a certain outcome. His lucidity and spirited ability to blunt the bullying invective of the attorney-general, Edward Coke, made it too difficult for the government to try and succeed in yoking Ralegh to the Bye plot, especially while public interest was high. Nor did they risk placing Cobham beside him to testify, for all he remained the Crown's only witness. On Cecil's orders it was Sir Walter Cope, a close associate of the minister, who led the search of Cobham's house in Blackfriars, looking for incriminating papers and seizing Cobham's servants. Nor was any spy for the government ever brought into court to testify against any of the accused. The difficulty with Cobham on trial was that he had already retracted earlier testimony and thus gave uncertainty a sharper edge. A public examination of him in such tense

Supporters of Arabella Stuart thought she had a better claim to the throne than James VI because she had been born in England. Some of the more moderate Catholics would have welcomed her accession as offering more tolerance to them

circumstances would very likely have rendered his evidence worthless in a confusing voiding of faltering denials from, as Ralegh charitably described him, 'a poor silly, base, dishonourable soul'. Indeed, as an accused it was Cobham who sought to implicate Lady Arabella, and the charges of complicity certainly required that she should deny such things. In fact she was there, observing and listening from a gallery, and the old Earl of Nottingham, seated beside her, rose to protest that on her hopes of salvation she had never meddled in any such matters. Sir Robert Cecil himself acknowledged that she was not in any way tainted by the plot, and that the letter broaching treason from Cobham she had put before the king. Nottingham as a friend of Ralegh (and father-in-law of Cobham) did venture to suggest that it might serve to bring the two men face to face. However the crown lawyers baulked at this civil notion and Ralegh was condemned as James intended since he had an eye on his fortune.[4] When Cobham and Grey were arraigned they too were condemned.

So the government now had a cluster of condemned men to deal with – priests and men of privilege. Clemency to all of them was not proper although Northumberland spoke to James on behalf of Ralegh and Cobham. Nor at the beginning of a reign was it suitable to have too much blood being shed. From his cell William Watson did send out an appeal, but it was not, as might have been expected, to the Catholic Earl of Worcester. Instead he wrote to William Herbert, Earl of Pembroke, because he knew how taken James was with the young man and he hoped the letter would be passed directly to the king.[5] But on 29 November, the day the Venetian embassy made their farewells to James, both priests were executed and were 'very bloodily handled'; neither claimed to be repentant in the manner that had become customary. As for George Brooke – he seems to have been the butt of a bitter little joke when executed. Sir John Harington, a friend of Cecil's, had told the Secretary that Brooke blamed him (Cecil) for his failure to become Master of the Hospital of St Cross in Winchester, and it was opposite this building that the execution took place. Writing to John Chamberlain, Dudley Carleton noted that when the executioner held up the severed head with the cry of 'God save the King', no one but the sheriff responded with the echoing cry.[6] So no applause, only silence for the removal of one of those who straddled the Bye and Main plots. Cobham, Grey and Ralegh remained, as did the lesser figure of Sir Griffin Markham, and on a day of atrocious weather a little after the execution of Brooke, it was Markham who was first escorted to the scaffold. The battle-scarred veteran was restless and declamatory, evidently expecting a last minute reprieve. It began to look as if that would come too late and though he regained some composure he had no last words prepared. The sheriff therefore halted proceedings and Markham was granted two hours in the great hall of the castle.

When Grey was brought to the scaffold his countenance was so cheerful 'that he seemed a dapper young bridegroom'. When he declared ringingly that he did not deserve to die the crowd may have anticipated a moment or two of high drama, but what they got was a dull interlude in the rain while for half an hour Grey prayed for the king's health. Then the sheriff again intervened and Grey was escorted to the castle as well. Finally Cobham was brought out, and Carleton evidently expected a farcical end for him, only again the sheriff held up the business, and this time both Grey and Markham were brought back to confront Cobham looking 'strange one upon the other, like men beheaded and met again in the other world'. The climax of the day came with the sheriff announcing the king's pardon. This brought hoots and cheers from the crowd which echoed round the town, while Ralegh, watching the scene and anticipating his own death the following Monday, must have 'had hammers working in his head to beat out the meaning of this stratagem'. In London the announcement from the throne stirred applause from those nearest the king and it made its way around the court. The reprieved men after had various fortunes. Grey remained in prison until his death in 1614; Cobham was imprisoned until shortly before his death in 1619, by which time Ralegh had been executed on the old conviction. As for Markham, he was held in prison for a short time, until paroled and exiled to the Low Countries. This routine is a very familiar one and certainly suggests that he went as a spy for Cecil even though he joined the 'English' regiment. Lady Markham evidently thought it was worth staying in England and she spent some time lobbying hard for the rehabilitation and return of her husband, until patience exhausted she ended up making a bigamous marriage.

Dudley Carleton made a mordant quip about the execution of Watson and Clarke when he noted that 'the priests led the dance'. Among Catholics abroad their fate seems to have elicited a certain grim relish. Robert Owen thought they had failed to obey their spiritual superiors and merited their fate. His brother Hugh writing to Captain Elyot thought it God's justice that those who had accused the Jesuits of being perturbators of kingdoms should be the first to offend against 'him whom themselves set up'. Even Clement VIII condemned the two priests without equivocation and even sent a secret envoy to the English court expressing his abhorrence of all acts of disloyalty. In addition he offered to withdraw any missionary from England and Wales who was unacceptable to the king and council. For a time James seemed to be benignly influenced by this gesture and as part of his coronation festivities allowed pardons to all Catholics who came forward to seek one. The momentum for a change seemed to be underlined by a meeting at some time between March and July 1603; Cecil met Sir Thomas Tresham, a prominent Catholic from one of the leading families of Northamptonshire, whose brother William had become a captain in the service of Spain. However, Sir Thomas himself was loyal, and a week before his coronation on St James' day, the king met him and a group of Catholics. For a time the fines were halted and the income from the two-thirds of goods and property fell sharply. Evidently James and his councillors, familiar and new, thought it politic to try to buy off opposition; and the shift may have tempted men like the exiled Stanley who had begun to hanker for his estates. Even so, in despatches from Brussels to Spain, James was still described as truly hostile to Jesuit sympathizers and Stanley himself at this time was a member of the archducal Council of War.

Early in July 1603, Stanley, Hugh Owen and Father Baldwin accompanied a young special messenger from England called Robert Spiller to a meeting with the new envoy of Spain to England, Juan de Tassis.[7] To try to avoid being observed by spies the four exiles arrived late at the ambassador's lodgings and Tassis wrote notes as they discussed conditions in England as well as the political leanings of Jacobean politicians. Essentially this aspect of the conversation was about who might usefully be bribed and who not. Robert Cecil was viewed as anti-Spanish, but Owen still hoped to see about James a cluster of royal councillors favouring Spain and Rome. For a clandestine mission to London to further this notion he selected Dr Robert Taylor, like Guy Fawkes a Yorkshireman, but one who had quit England after the accession of Elizabeth. During this visit Taylor had aid and advice from Anthony Skinner, at one time a servant of Cardinal Allen who had thoughtfully excluded him from the Jesuits. Skinner's career in the Spanish navy had also been cut short, apparently because of sea-sickness, but he did receive a pension of 40 escudos when in the Low Countries.[8] As yet unable to settle he chose to return to London where his income was supposedly some 3,000 escudos (£750 then, or circa £37,500 today). Given the sometimes testy rivalry between the spy services of the Earl of Essex and the Cecils in the early 1590s after the death of Walsingham, it is not surprising that Skinner was soon under arrest. Imprisoned and tortured he confessed a part in a plot (later retracted) to murder Elizabeth, and Richard Verstegen, in the newsletter he produced, reported Skinner's trial in August 1592. Although condemned the payment of £500 by his friends led to the substitution of a prison sentence, and since Sir Thomas Heneage was his saviour we may infer that the young man was then recruited as a spy – Heneage having taken on some of the intelligence work of the late Walsingham. Skinner's sentence may have been shortened by apostasy, and certainly he gained the confidence of the capable (if rather expensive) English government spy based in Antwerp, William Sterrell (alias H. St. Main or Robert Robinson). He had fairly frequent dealings with Hugh Owen, and on three occasions he asked that Skinner be sent to Liège for meetings.

At the time of Dr Taylor's secret visit to London, Father Henry Garnet, who met him, wrote to Robert Persons decrying the stupidity of Watson and Clarke. Persons wrote back on 6 July in a gloomy frame of mind, lamenting missed opportunities in the previous decade, and offering no hope that James might yet be converted. He did not think anything dramatic or of galvanizing immediacy could be done, and he simply advised those who resisted diaspora to hold tight and 'to expect the event of things'. The 'retrospective' and the letter Persons addressed to James in October 1603 indicate that for an option he still had not given up the idea of resistance and that it was simply a matter of seizing the moment. 'This is not to say that in 1603 [he] was threatening to blow up the king and Parliament. But it does suggest that Parsons (sic) wanted James to know that he and others were watching . . . very carefully and that they intended to leave all options open.'[9] Persons was a constant source of irritating propaganda and the English government could not ignore his connections. Early on James sent the ageing and retired spy Sir Anthony Standen on a diplomatic mission to the Duke of Lorraine, to Venice and then to the Grand Duke of Tuscany. The sometime intelligencer made the curious mistake, for a man with his past, of being indiscreet, communicating with Persons, and indicating when finally he got to Rome that he was acting on behalf of Queen Anne whose Catholic leanings were growing. Sir Thomas Parry intercepted mail from Standen who committed the sin of being candid in a letter, and so it was that Cecil learnt Standen was returning with a rosary from the Pope to the queen. James was incensed at the opinion that he could be converted through the agency of a woman and on his return Standen was arrested and placed in the Tower for some ten months.

On 19 February 1604 James protested 'his utter detestation of their superstitious religion'. So he and his bishops agreed. In asserting and defending the true faith there was the inevitable conclusion that all others were false, heretical and hence condemned. The rider to that was that they should be suppressed. So in his arguments against the Roman Church and its doctrines he followed the lead of Elizabethan divines in regarding those who were elected Pope as embodying Antichrist. This brittle antipathy was reflected in such books as George Downame's *A Treatise affirming the Pope to be Antechrist* (1603) or Robert Abbot's *Anti-Christi Demonstratio* of the same year. The tedium of such arguments was not felt then, moulding as they did the thoughts of salvation of the sixteenth and seventeenth centuries. It was the Anglo-Catholicism of Whitgift and Lancelot Andrewes that James was quick to defend because personally he hated the Puritans more than he did the Catholics. Even so it was the missal and its threat that immediately seized his attention. The powerful surge of the Counter-Reformation was unmistakable, and Catholics had a particular advantage over the Puritans – a centralized organization and a man at the top whose authority was pan-European (even partially global) and temporal; one whose claims, in fact, no 'supreme governor' could ever allow.[10]

This led James on 22 February 1604 to take up the challenge with a proclamation that ordered all Jesuits and seminary priests to leave the country before the opening of Parliament on 19 March. On the same day the recusancy fine was again activated and by the following month the direction was obviously heading towards a reimposition of the Elizabethan code. The Bye plot, ineffective and blundering, had indicated the extraordinary speed with which optimism on both sides had decayed. On 16 July a priest, John Sugar, and his harbourer Robert Grissold were executed at Warwick in the locale that became crucial to the gunpowder plotters. Grissold's brother John was one of Garnet's servants, using the alias James Johnson. The following year he was in charge at White Webbs and was subsequently almost racked to death. It may have been a matter of zeal in local magistrates rather than the government in London, but then in August two laymen were executed at Lancaster at about the time James was staying with the Catholic Lord Mordaunt at Drayton (Northants). The hospitality must have been exceptional but it did not prevent Mordaunt from having frequent contacts with the plotters. It did, however, delay James's return to London even though there had arrived Juan de Velasco, Constable of Castile and Duke of Frias, the representative of Philip III, to sign the formal peace agreement negotiated between England and Spain (Scotland had never been at war) in eighteen sessions between 20 May and 6 July. It was while gathering himself for the crossing to Dover that the Constable had been visited in April by Thomas Winter, whose account records that one of his objectives was to ram home the case of English Catholicism and so influence the negotiations that were held at Somerset House. The meeting had been arranged by Hugh Owen, but it proved to be a distinct failure. Even so, Winter did not totally waste his time for he renewed his acquaintance with Guy Fawkes and managed to persuade him of the utility of a visit to England in May. Sir William Stanley was also consulted when in camp at Ostend and he recommended Fawkes while still deprecating any project during the time of peace negotiations. Winter told Stanley that nothing had been decided and repeated this to Fawkes when he met him in Dunkirk. Even at this distance the assertion seems hollow.

The hopes of Philip III, his Council of State and his negotiators who sat on one side of the turkey-carpeted table opposite the leading figures of Jacobean politics led by Cecil, the hopes of a peace, were strikingly fulfilled. One curiosity did fall – the notion of the strongly anti-Spanish Prince Henry marrying an Infanta, although the gift of a Spanish horse and embroidered velvet tackle did please the young man.[11] In his disinclination to marry outside his religion Henry was only following his father's advice, though it sits oddly with the comically desperate efforts to secure later the Spanish match for his other son. As for the English Catholics, nervously expectant, their case was nudged into limbo and proved to be the great topic on which the diplomats chose to remain mute. Any covert expressions of mild sympathy for their situation by Northampton (who like Cecil spoke Spanish) was more than offset by the stern attitude of the House of Commons, where any relaxation of statute and its enforcement was regarded with abhorrence. They did not want Catholicism treated as 'tolerated vice'. Indeed, after only four sessions of the Somerset House conference, a bill requiring the imposition of statutes (of which there were plenty) against Jesuits, priests, recusants etc., not only re-enacted the Elizabethan code but extended it to penalize those who sent children or adults overseas to study at the seminaries, and those who remained in such institutions. In September, while the Constable was slowly returning to Spain via Flanders, a commission was created to execute the laws for the banishment of Jesuits and seminary priests. The government ignored their protests and also began to enforce the recusancy fines upon the laity, more strictly than they might have done because James needed money to placate courtiers and servants. Royal extravagance and failures in collection of taxes would eventually lead to a crisis, and in the meantime the archduke hoped to exploit matters by seeking to buy the cautionary towns in the territory of the Estates General.

The prophetic analysis of Hugh Owen with regard to James was being fulfilled.[12] He noted the onerous conditions of his co-religionists in England, and he assumed (or was told by his couriers) that the plot first talked of earlier in the year was advancing. Cecil's spy Thomas Allyson, who was in the Low Countries about the time the peace was concluded, reported hints from Owen about the Infanta's claim; angry references to Cecil, Bancroft and Sir John Popham, and venom directed at James. Allyson followed this a little later by offering to procure for Cecil a copy of the plot against James drawn up by Owen and his Jesuit friends, with reasons advanced for the archdukes, the Pope and Philip III to reject the peace treaty. The exiled spy master evidently had hopes for a breakdown in Anglo-Scottish relations leading to civil war over the question of union, with the consequent intervention of Spain. In England there were signs of real disappointment in James and a growing sense of despondent unease among Catholics. A minor revolt broke out in Herefordshire during the summer, and

At the time of the plot's discovery it was widely believed that Thomas Percy had written the warning letter to Monteagle. The death of Percy at Holbeach prevented further examination of this intriguing point

there were rumours of guns, armour and horses being collected for some violent activity. Like all such rumours the numbers tended to multiply in the telling. In September, twenty-one priests and three laymen were banished, and the notorious case against old Thomas Pound(e) reached star chamber in December. Since the arrival of Campion in England whom he had befriended, Pound had spent much of the last twenty-five years in gaols and was arraigned at this time for protesting against the cruelty of the law and recent executions. The new sentence he received was bizarre; one ear was to be severed in London and the other in Lancaster, while his term in prison was extended to coincide with the length of his life. In addition, a fine of £1,000 was imposed. The mutilation was later commuted to standing in the pillory in each place for one day, his ears nailed but not cut off.

Rational men, men hitherto of discretion, began to fume at James for shifting policy, but then in both Scotland and England policy demanded that he should in the main stick to the religion of his tutors rather than that of his mother. One of those who felt particularly aggrieved was Thomas Percy, who seems to have had an over-measure in his personality of Percy eccentricity. The physical markers of companion mental instability were there – surges of wild energy subsiding into sloth; insomnia and a skin disorder so acute 'he could not endure any shirt but of the finest holland or cambric'. Percy had shifted to Catholicism at about the same time as Robert Catesby, and fired with the emphatic enthusiasm of a proselyte had gone privately in 1603 to James at Holyrood as messenger for the Earl of Northumberland, hoping to draw from the king a promise of favour to the Catholics on his accession. It was reported that Thomas Percy had been assured of an accommodation that would allow them to worship discreetly and have their grievances amended. James afterwards would only deny this and given the recorded quaintness of his spoken English the possibilities for misunderstanding on both sides were very great. Probably he gave what he considered an airy (and suitably vague) assurance, and some colour may have been given to Percy's confidence by his own appointment to a coveted vacancy in the gentlemen pensioners in ordinary, a privileged royal bodyguard. With the outbreak of persecution Percy felt horribly like a dupe and presented a remonstrance to James to which no reply was given. His broad contempt for Scots easily encompassed the Stuart, and it was an unsettlingly potent view collectively held in England by a majority.[13] As yet the simultaneous stirrings in the country had only parochial meanings, but given the atmosphere of ill-directed animosity in collision with repression, Robert Catesby who was to lead the gunpowder plotters identified an opportunity already hopelessly fluffed by the Bye plotters. What he settled upon was on a far more destructive and grandiose scale. How he tried to destroy the English government, the Anglo-Scottish royal family and the laws of the land, and why he failed, forms the next section of this book.

FOUR

The Gentlemen of the Sword

Shaped to counter the full tide of the influence of the Counter-Reformation, the religious policies of late Elizabethan England guaranteed conflict. The regime of Burghley and his fellow councillors was successful in putting down discontent, but it required violent counter-measures against dissidents of varying persuasions. Those who escaped abroad were sometimes jammed together, young men in the seminaries, restless and angry, capable of ill-judged mayhem when given the chance. To clamp down on any such efforts the great men of the privy council began to recognize the utility of intelligence operations, and as each plot against Elizabeth was uncovered, however fantastical, like the Squire's plot, the rhetoric of denunciation by the discoverers grew more heightened and venomous. The treasons involved men from a variety of backgrounds whose combative inclinations were ill-sorted, unsteady and often lacking sense. Tense energy could also be distorted by cupshot camaraderie since London was crammed with taverns and ordinaries where men might meet in hired rooms. An estimate of the frequency of taverns has suggested an average of one to every eighteen houses. The taverns could be very large and the Bear in Westminster and the Angel near the Tower both had twenty-one rooms. Ordinaries were originally eating houses and there were various grades. In the twelvepenny ordinary the men of fashion took their meals and later played cards or dice. Even wealthy residents in London like Anthony Babington kept company in such places and met his fellow conspirators in them because 'there were innkeepers who catered for the numerous Catholic gentry'.

Drunkenness was an accepted habit of the day; affrays in the street were common. On the night of 18 March 1600 the unenviably nicknamed 'Pox' Baynham (Sir Edmund Baynham), one of a number of young rips who swarmed around the Earl of Essex, led such an affray in the Mermaid. At midnight they 'cast off their cloaks and upper garments', drew rapiers and daggers and marched through the streets until they came upon the bemused watch. After a scuffle (and no recorded injuries, or injuries worth recording perhaps) they were overcome and locked in the Counter prison to sober up. Baynham was in a belligerent mood and when the story reached Elizabeth (who must have wearied of these performances) she set the case before the star chamber, 'for the more and exemplar punishment of so great and outrageous disorder'. The rioters at first denied the charges, but when brought before the court on 6 July 'confessed their faults and submitted themselves to the court and proved that all was done in the drink and heat'. Each man was fined £200 and imprisoned, but Baynham was evidently free to join the Essex revolt, an even more 'outrageous disorder'. His plea this time was ignorance and the sentence death, but once again he was pardoned (in August 1601) after paying Ralegh a large sum. Yet as the leader of the so-called 'damned crew', Baynham had learned nothing about civic decorum, and when Elizabeth died he was briefly sent to the Marshalsea prison by the privy council for declaring that James VI was a schismatic 'and that he would not acknowledge him as King'.

After Essex had led his followers in the miserable skirmish that ended his career, some sixty-six gentlemen were imprisoned and fifteen of them were suspected Catholics. Sir Griffin Markham was among them and fetched up in the Fleet; Robert Catesby, who was wounded, was sent to the Tower and might have been executed then had not Elizabeth been moved to save a very personable young man from a premature death. Instead she substituted a heavy fine of 4,000 marks (getting on for £3,000), and Catesby had the mortification of seeing 1,200 marks of his bestowed on Francis Bacon who was always short of money. To raise such a very large sum Catesby was forced to sell Chastleton, his manor in

Personable and winning in many ways, the young Earl of Essex, Robert Devereux's political sense was often wildly adrift, and it cost him his life prematurely in 1601

Oxfordshire, and for this employed the good offices of his friend Thomas Percy, steward or agent to the Earl of Northumberland. When Catesby left the Tower he still had his head, but no inclination to use it for sober reflection, and his immoderate actions and vexatious losses caused no loss of esteem for him among certain of his contemporaries. It was noted by John Gerard that Catesby was 'respected in all companies of such as are counted there swordsmen or men of action, that few were in the opinions of most men preferred before him and he increased much his acquaintance and friends.' The gunpowder plot was Catesby's conspiracy and this has led certain Catholic writers on the period to view him with morbid suspicion. Hilaire Belloc sternly called him 'a doubtful character' and wondered if he had betrayed his own cause to the government.[1] More recently Father Francis Edwards, SJ, has suggested something along the same lines, and colours it with the thought that having been obliged to sell Chastleton and live with his mother at Ashby St Legers, he would not have been inclined to embark on a new episode that, if it failed, threatened total ruin.[2] Edwards also cites a deathbed confession by one George Bartlet, apparently a servant of Catesby, that his master went to Salisbury House several nights before the discovery 'and was always brought privately in at a back door'. This is thin stuff, too remote from many details available in other sources of a dynamic enthusiast.

Robert Catesby was born in 1573; tradition has it at Bushwood Hall, near Lapworth, some eleven miles from Stratford-upon-Avon.[3] It was the favoured residence of his devout Catholic father, Sir William Catesby, always in trouble as a noted recusant. Robert was the only surviving son of Sir William and Lady Anne, the daughter of Sir Robert Throckmorton of Coughton. They sent him for a time to Gloucester Hall (now Worcester College) Oxford, favoured by the recusant gentry who took their sons away after residence of a year or two in order to escape the obligations of the oath of supremacy. There is a suggestion that the young man may have gone on to Douai before marrying the Protestant Catherine Leigh, daughter of the influential Protestant Sir Thomas Leigh of Stoneleigh, in 1592. The Chastleton parish register has an entry for their son Robert who was baptized on 11 November 1595. While his wife lived she seems to have prompted good behaviour in her husband, a steadying influence that was sadly lost by her death after the birth of their second son. The boy Robert was a mere child of eight when he was betrothed to a daughter of Thomas Percy, an arrangement which strengthened an old friendship, but which might have been curtailed if Catherine Catesby had lived longer. The death of old Sir William Catesby in 1598 took away the remaining person who might have tempered his son's headstrong disposition. When Chastleton was sold and he lived with his widowed mother in her house there were quarrels as he sold reversionary property, since he had not only the huge post-Essex revolt fine to pay, but was funding Jesuit missionaries and other priests. He was now deeply in with the other religious malcontents, having meditated a powder plot to get rid of Elizabeth. In the circumstances Catesby did what seemed best to him to advance the cause of militant Catholicism. In doing so he swept aside the nervous reflections of many by his physical presence and the gusty force of his character. Even his mother failed to curb him despite her perturbations – but when does a man afire (symbolized in his constant choice of red clothes) ever listen with attention to 'wise' counsel from a powerless woman, even one who had known him longer and perhaps better than anyone? He loved her and she loved him with all his manifest faults, but however she strove she could not save him from himself – his other self than son. Was he in ignoring her allowing himself the unspoken privilege of punishing her for some fault unknown to us, or a sin, as he saw it, in her own past conduct? Had she perhaps thought to remarry immediately after the death of Sir William, so arousing bemused distress touched with rage in her only son Robin? Remarriage would have set her estate and income out of her son's grasp and likely precipitated the collapse of all his well-resourced pre-plot clandestine efforts. Somewhere here is the teasingly vague but insistent sense that Catesby and his mother provided the inspiration for Hamlet and Gertrude, in the same way that the parochial story of Brian Annesley, gentleman pensioner to Queen Elizabeth, and his daughters may have been the seed for genius to create at length the universal tragedy of *King Lear*.

Perhaps in about June 1603 Catesby was not entirely surprised when Thomas Percy visited Ashby St Legers, plunged into his friend's presence and began to rage against James's perfidy. (What did Lady Anne make of this?) Over the porch at the manor there is still an ancient half-timbered room called the 'Plot Room', and this may perhaps have been the place where Percy declared he would kill the king with his own hands. Catesby in the moment responded to this coolly: 'No, no, Tom, thou shalt not venture to small purpose, but if thou wilt be a traitor thou shalt be to some great advantage.' As Percy took interest and subsided, Catesby added: 'I am thinking of a most sure way and I will soon let thee know what it is.' This is the first definite hint of the inception of the conspiracy which was evidently not yet in its final form. He agreed with Percy that the king was far removed in his actions from what they had hoped, but he still needed to consult with a friend of less raw judgment and impetuosity. At Allhallowtide (31 October) Catesby sent a messenger to the brothers Thomas and Robert Winter at Huddington, asking that they meet him in London; the cousins needed to talk. Robert Winter, the elder of the two, simply declined and probably dissuaded Thomas, who later wrote: 'I desired him to excuse me; for I found myself not very well disposed; and which had happened to me never before, returned the messenger without my company. Shortly, I received another letter, in any wise to come.' Robert Catesby could be an importunate relation.

Thomas Winter had for years been concerned to join plans for Catholic relief, and had a reputation for being careful and considerate. He had been a soldier in the Low Countries and was also 'a reasonable good scholar' with a knowledge of several languages. He may have been converted to Catholicism then, and in 1600 he made a pilgrimage to Rome for the Holy Year celebrations. In 1602 he went to Spain in company with Father Greenway (the alias of Father Oswald Tesimond who had been at school with Guy Fawkes). They went as the agents of Father Garnet, Robert Catesby and Francis Tresham, on a mission funded by Tresham's cousin, Lord Monteagle, who employed Winter as his secretary. The introductions to the Spanish were done by the Jesuit Father Cresswell, ex-rector of the English College in Rome and now charged to supervise English Jesuits in Spain.[4] It was at his Madrid house that Winter met a relation-by-marriage,

Christopher Wright and Guy Fawkes himself. He had fought for the archdukes in the siege of Calais, but subsequently found it difficult to make a living as a mercenary. It was Cresswell who urged the visitors' case to Spanish officials and there was a promise of financial aid plus military support from Stanley's regiment in an invasion to coincide with a rising in England. Elizabeth's death spoilt this plot so it might be described as her final act of policy on behalf of her country. Philip III preferred the chances of a stable peace with James, and the lack of unity at home and abroad settled any prospect of the English Catholics managing to snatch definitely advantageous terms for themselves before James trundled into England. This woeful failure on their part was what eventually brought the pro-Spanish exiles so close into the counsels of the gunpowder plotters once their relief at Elizabeth's death had subsided into gloomy ruminations on the future. In the meantime it was Father Watson and the 'seculars' who attempted to seize the king and the initiative that summer of 1603.

When the messenger from Catesby arrived urging him to visit, being no fool Thomas Winter surely suspected some enterprise more serious than cards or hunting. Winter was a man of the world and his generous attachment to his cousin did not blind him to Catesby's principal personality defect – a soaring optimism yoked to unrestrained ambition. When the second summons arrived for Winter he overcame his reluctance and went. 'At the second summons I presently came up and found him with Mr John Wright at Lambeth where he broke with me how necessary it was not to forsake our country, for he knew I had a resolution to go over [i.e. to the Spanish Netherlands], but to deliver her from the servitude in which she remained, or at least to assist her with my utmost endeavours.' This pressure to stay ruffled Winter a little and he replied that he had 'hazarded his life upon far lighter terms, and now would not refuse any good occasion wherein he might do service to the Catholic Cause; but for himself he knew no mean probable to succeed.' Not much to encourage his listeners in such plain speaking, especially with its hint of rebuke for Wright's notorious readiness to draw sword at any opportunity. Clearly Catesby wanted Wright there as an engaged witness and Winter's response showed that he had noted the intention of snaring him in a scheme. So Catesby was forced to drop his sidelong approach and made a quick, confident appeal. 'He had thought of a way to deliver them from all their bonds and without any foreign help to replant again the Catholic religion.' There was a pause charged with some anticipation of what was to come. Catesby and Wright scrutinized their silent guest and then the former uttered the crucial sentence of this encounter – the intention was to blow up the Parliament house with gunpowder. Winter's first spontaneous response was a gasp of amazement rather than horror. He stared at Catesby who added 'In that place have they done us all the mischief and perchance God hath designed that place for their punishment.'[5]

Reasonable incredulity at the fearsome nature of the proposal gradually subsided as they discussed the matter. Winter did not immediately withdraw by declaring it a monstrous absurdity. Having once been a soldier calculating risks, he fell back on his practical experience to see if he could begin to weigh up the chances of success or failure. The notion did strike at the root and would cause general confusion and changes; but if it failed, as did almost all similar schemes, then the scandal would be a great grief to their cause, 'their religion would be injured, and not only enemies, but friends with good reason condemn them'. Catesby answered with that commonplace response of all who regard horror as a purification – only he gave it a medicinal slant. 'The nature of the disease required so sharp a remedy.'[6] He asked Winter if he would give his consent and despite the countervailing pressures he still felt his reply was 'Yes, in this or what else soever, if he resolved upon it I would venture my life.' So Thomas Winter, who was not a religious zealot, gave his initial consent (which proved to be binding), while still hoping that Catholics might yet benefit if relief could be procured by the peaceful intervention of Philip III. Catesby was no doubt a sceptic on this point, but wisely allowed that they would 'leave no peaceable and quiet way untried . . . you shall go over and inform the Constable Don Juan de Velasco, of the state of Catholics in England, entreating him to solicit his Majesty, at his coming hither, that the Penal Laws may be recalled and we admitted into the rank of his other subjects.' Winter who spoke Spanish well, readily agreed. Catesby then artfully nudged the matter in the direction of his own plan by requesting Winter to 'bring over some confident (that is trustworthy) gentleman, such as you shall understand best for this business' – by which he meant mining, and so named Guy Fawkes.

The meeting with the Constable, as we have seen, was a polite deadlock. Hugh Owen had warned that this would be the outcome, and in conversation with Winter touched on the second reason for his being in the Low Countries: the availability to any rising in England of Guy Fawkes whom he had met in Spain garlanded with 'good commendations'. Owen did praise the skill of Fawkes as a siege master and promised that if Winter did not get to see him – Fawkes being then in Brussels – 'he would send him shortly after to England'. Most of those considering the personnel of the gunpowder plot have assumed that the pull of his religion was enough for the professional soldier. This seems very unlikely since he had quit England in his twenty-first year, having sold his inheritance, to fight in Spanish service and would require something substantial to induce his return. Fawkes by this time had become by choice a rootless mercenary soldier, that would be reason enough. At the same time Winter wanted an informed opinion of another soldier on Fawkes's merits and so he went to Ostend for the meeting with Sir William Stanley. Fawkes's commander was asked about his 'sufficiency in the wars' and since the Spanish service gave a notable training in military engineering at that time, Stanley was able to give 'very good commendations of him'. Winter was preparing to return to England when Fawkes arrived in the town and the two men talked there and further up the coast in Dunkirk. It seems likely that Fawkes was nudged towards acquiescence by Stanley, and two days later he did follow Winter down the coast and consented to return with him. Winter remained quite cautious in his briefing, saying no more than that there was 'a resolution to do somewhat in England, if the peace with Spain helped us not, but as yet resolved upon nothing'. It would certainly be very surprising if Fawkes's resolution was not assisted by a cash reward.

After sailing back to England, Winter and Fawkes took a two-pair of oars at Greenwich and rowed up to the Lambeth house where they were received by

Catesby. Naturally his first question was 'What news from the Constable?' Winter's reply was clipped and sardonic – 'Good words.' Not knowing Fawkes otherwise than by report Catesby held back somewhat in his company, but while waiting for the arrival of Thomas Percy in town he did engage Fawkes provisionally for service. Early in May Percy did arrive; he could handily claim business over the rents of his employer Northumberland to cover the conspiratorial aspect of his visit. He saluted the company – Catesby, Winter, John Wright and Fawkes – and asked vehemently: 'Shall we always, gentlemen, talk and never do anything?' The others looked at Catesby who then took Percy aside and explained that a scheme was being considered. They were set to meet within two or three days to bind themselves by an oath of secrecy, and this took place in a lodging belonging to a Mrs Herbert in Butcher's Row behind St Clement's Dane church. In an upper room, probably a garret reached by a trap-door 'upon a Primer' each swore the oath generally supposed to have been as follows: 'Ye shall swear by the Blessed Trinity and by the Sacrament ye now prepare to receive never to disclose directly or indirectly by word or circumstances the matter that shall be proposed to you to keep secret nor desist from the execution thereof until the rest shall give you leave.'[7] After this they went into an adjoining room where the Jesuit priest Father John Gerard, ignorant of their intentions, was vested and ready to say the mass and they made their communion. Retiring back to their empty room then, Catesby disclosed their purpose to Thomas Percy, while Winter and John Wright told Fawkes.

As a first step the conspirators needed to find a house to rent hard by the cluster of old buildings known collectively as the Houses of Parliament. Their choice came down to one (or rather part of one) standing near the Prince's Chamber, and on the side towards the river. It was then in the possession of Henry Ferrers of Baddesley Clinton, the tenant of John Whynniard, yeoman of his Majesty's Wardrobe of the Beds. In his first effort for the operation Thomas Percy was selected to take the house in his own name, using the simple pretence that his position in the King's gentleman pensioners to which he was appointed on 9 June, required him to reside periodically in the ambit of the court. The bargaining for the house was eventually completed on 24 May 1604, St Robert's Day, after a 'long suit' by Percy, and pressing requests by people connected to the Earl of Northumberland – Dudley Carleton and John Hippesley.[8] But nothing yet could be done there because the premises were being used for important government business. The Scottish commissioners appointed by James to consider his great plan for the Union of Scotland and England were ensconced in it for several months. In the meantime, so that the flare of initial energy of the plot was not fruitlessly snuffed, the conspirators hired Catesby's lodgings in Lambeth, conveniently opposite to Whynniard's block, but on the south bank of the Thames. It was there that they laid up a store of gunpowder, wood and other combustibles. At an appropriate moment these could be moved at night by boat; and in the meantime a friend of Kit Wright – John's brother – was taken on to watch the items as they lay in store. Robert Keyes was a Jesuit convert whose father had been a Protestant clergyman at Staveley, Derbyshire, while his mother was a Catholic relative of Lady Ursula Babthorpe. His wife was governess at

The Houses of Parliament in the time of James I

Turvey (Bedfordshire) to the children of the Catholic Lord Mordaunt, and since the Keyes family was not well off it seems likely that Catesby paid him and then took him into the plot on the conviction that he was 'a trusty honest man'.[9]

The commission on Union completed its work by 6 December 1604, and less than a week later the conspirators were back in possession of the house. By Christmas, these gentlemen, so unused to hard physical labour, but now galvanized by their mission, had tunnelled from their starting point to the wall they had to breach. They took a festive break then, no doubt glad to ease the blisters they had accumulated in a short time. When they set about the wall they were presented with a severe physical challenge, since it was stone and several feet thick. Eating from a store of eggs, dried meat and the like (where did they get their drinking water?), so as not to arouse suspicions in the crowded neighbourhood by frequent comings and goings of prepared food, they continued to work in very cramped conditions that took their toll. Up to this time it had been Catesby, Percy, Fawkes, Thomas Winter and John Wright who had done the labouring and maintained a watch. But not enough was being achieved and Keyes had to be brought in, which meant the gunpowder too. At this time they had about twenty barrels and this was now stored either in Percy's lodgings or in an outhouse belonging to it. A fortnight after Candlemas, Christopher Wright was also brought in, but between January 1605

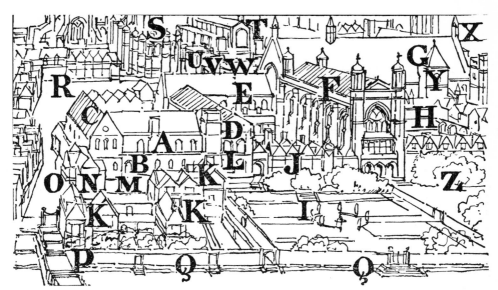

Houses of Parliament in the time of James I
A. The House of Lords.   B.   Chamber under the House of Lords called 'Guy Fawkes' Cellar.'
C. The Prince's Chamber.   D. The Painted Chamber.   E. The 'White Hall' or Court of
Requests.   F. The House of Commons (formerly St Stephen's Chapel).   G. Westminster Hall.
H. St Stephen's Cloisters, converted into houses for the Tellers of the Exchequer.   I. Garden of the
Old Palace (afterwards called 'Cotton Garden').   J. House built on the site of the Chapel of
'Our Lady of the Pew' (called later 'Cotton House').   K. Houses built upon ruins of the walls of
the Old Palace.   L. Vault under the Painted Chamber.   M. Yard or Court into which a doorway
opened from Guy Fawkes' Cellar.   N. Passage leading from the same Yard or Court into
Parliament Place.   O. Parliament Place.   P. Parliament Stairs (formerly called 'The
Queen's Bridge').   Q. The River Thames.   R. Old Palace Yard.   S. Westminster Abbey.
T. St Margaret's Church.   U. V. W. Buildings of the Old Palace called 'Heaven' (or 'Paradise'),
'Hell,' and 'Purgatory.'   X. New Palace Yard.   Y. Bell Tower of St Stephen's.   Z. The
Speaker's Garden.

and the middle of March they had got perhaps halfway through. It was undoubtedly an effort that generated noise, and unless Fawkes had rigged sound baffles there must have been a real fear that some day a nosey neighbour would seek out the source.* After all, as it has been pointed out in previous studies of the plot, there were people living in the part of the property not let to the conspirators, and they were hemmed in by houses of the Keeper of the Wardrobe, auditors and tellers of the Exchequer and other such officials. There were also tradesmen and workmen constantly employed close to where the

---

* The ability to mine silently had been claimed many years before by Leonardo da Vinci in his famous letter to Lodovico Sforza.

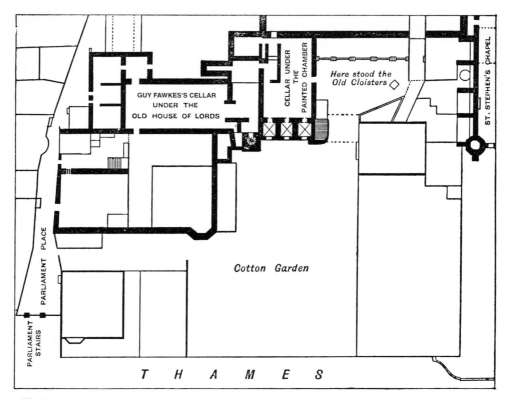

The last minute discovery of the gunpowder plot exacerbated the great fear that Catholics might through force or guile destroy the Protestant monarchy. Such a notion survived throughout the seventeenth century

work went on, and yet no quizzical eye spotted evidence of soil or stone. A solution to this is suggested in later prints of the environs which always show clear evidence of demolition and rebuilding, with casual heaps of timber and stone. Given the age of many of these buildings such work cannot have been rare in the early seventeenth century. Indeed, the other Robert of the gunpowder plot – Robert Cecil, soon to be Earl of Salisbury – was a demolisher and rebuilder on a grand scale. And if anyone troubled to ask what was going on the plotters could simply say essential repairs caused by destabilized foundations – the result of seepages from the Thames.

FIVE

The Hand of Providence

The physical effort of mining in a confined space was overwhelming the small group. Empowered by the others to use their discretion in bringing in further hands to the plot, Catesby and Thomas Percy sent off letters to Robert Winter of Huddington, and to his brother-in-law, John Grant, a wealthy squire who lived at Norbrook, an old manor house some five miles from Stratford. They were requested to meet their brother Thomas Winter and their kinsman Catesby, a meeting that took place in January 1605 at the Catherine Wheel inn in Oxford. Robert Winter and John Grant took the oath binding them to secrecy before Catesby revealed the intention. According to his trial testimony Robert Winter, who was a more peaceable character than his brother, asked why such a dangerous project was envisaged when (as he thought), it was 'impossible to take any effect without either foreign aid or some great men at home to join therein'. Catesby brushed these objections aside and said that 'for great men he knew none he durst trust'. Winter also took the view that like most plots before, discovery was inevitable and unless James himself was extraordinarily charitable it would scandalize all other Catholics and ruin those involved – a fact of some importance to Robert Winter who was not only the owner of large estates in Worcestershire, but also the son-in-law of Sir John Talbot of Grafton, the largest landholder in the county. Despite the presence of his brother the scepticism of Robert Winter was undiminished and he held back from joining the plotters at this time.

Not so John Grant, who had previously been involved in the Essex revolt and was married to Dorothy, the sister of the Winters.[1] A much more bellicose individual, Grant had a reputation for resisting government searchers when they descended on his strongly-walled property to pry for incriminating evidence. According to his contemporary, Father John Gerard, Grant gleefully heaped indignities on the pursuivants and they learned to stay away 'unless they brought store of help with them'. Doubtless one or two fetched up in the moat. Catesby wanted more men on site to dig but neither Robert Winter nor Grant seem to have moved south, perhaps because the timing of Parliament's sessions had been altered, prorogued from 7 February to 3 October (the day Thomas Winter was sent to watch the ceremony). Presumably the diggers had a day off on 7 February since the Lords met that day and aside from ceremonial matters they conducted, too, a little business, including the introduction of Lord Denny and the reading of his writ of summons. 'The Moles that first underwent these underminings were all grounded Schollers of the Romish Schoole', but they seem to have been

A participant in the Essex Rebellion, John Grant was well known to the government as a turbulent individual

surprisingly haphazard in their knowledge of the buildings about them and more specifically the object of their intentions – the House of Lords. In part this was probably due to a lack of plans for them to consult and the wilful ways of early builders when confronted with a problem of construction. The other factor, harder to calculate but impossible now to overlook, was that they were all gentlemen without any training in mining, demolition or understanding spatial relationships. Detailed planning applications to councils today often mystify the layman who has inadequate expertise in preparing a critique of such plans. The labourers then 'in their Vault of Villainy' operated more in hope than many writers have been willing to acknowledge, since whatever one's sympathies, it suggests an amateurishness on their part that seems to detract in some way from the desperate seriousness of their operation. They fumbled in the dark, no doubt unwilling to acknowledge their blithe ignorance because that was too dispiriting, and it made all their efforts so far seem lame. Even the man credited with the most skills in the matter of mining – Guy Fawkes – did not realize that their exit would not be immediately beneath the chamber of the peers. Hence their agitation, verging on panic, when they heard a strange overhead rushing sound that none of them could with any confidence identify to the satisfaction of the group. Before they could risk proceeding someone had to be delegated to go above to find out the source. In the event it was Fawkes himself who went, probably because he was the least likely to be recognized, and his later testimony suggests that it was only then that the calculations of proximities were recognized as faulty. There was a large space above where they were labouring, a so-called 'cellar', although it comprised the ground floor of the building and was itself beneath the chamber of the House of Lords. According to a measurement given in a volume published some two hundred years after the events being described, the space was 77 feet long, 24 feet 4 inches wide and 10 feet high, having originally served as a kitchen for the palace, but by 1605 it did function in part as a cellar might, since some of the space was given over to coal storage – a privilege that was rented out to a London coal merchant. It was the noise of the stock being removed that caused the alarums below, until Fawkes returned (I suggest with a rare grin on his face) to report that the tenant's widow, Ellen Bright, was selling off the stocks of coal, thus vacating the area at a crucial time. Curious when it was winter and there were working fire-places in the house. It cannot have taken the miners long to recognize that relief of their calloused hands and aching limbs was at hand. All they had to do was rent the space, to which no one paid any attention, and Thomas Percy set about obtaining the lease from Whynniard, but as ever the situation was a little more complicated than had first been thought. According to later testimony by Mrs Whynniard, Ellen Bright only had the lease indirectly through a man called Skinner, and while it is a fairly common name it would be interesting to know if he was in any way related to Anthony Skinner. Whatever the case the naturally voluble Percy was not deflected and the plotters had the space from 25 March 1605.[2]

So by a lucky coincidence (or something more sinister?) they had a depot for the gunpowder. Historians of the plot generally do not say much about this critical component of the scheme besides noting it had a tendency to dampness that reduced its efficiency. Long known as a simple mixture, gunpowder dated back to the thirteenth century. Its origin is obscure, but out of the controversies which have raged around its first manufacture, the name of Roger Bacon stands pre-eminent as the progenitor of English gunpowder which from the early medieval period onwards consisted of an intimate mixture of saltpetre, charcoal and sulphur in varying proportions according to the predilection of the powder maker.[3] The earliest form of gunpowder, known as serpentine, suffered from serious drawbacks, the chief of which was indeed its ability to absorb moisture owing to the hygroscopic nature of saltpetre. The solution to this was so-called corned powder, made in definite grains and known from some time in the fifteenth century; it was less susceptible to damp; did not stratify during transport and weight for weight produced more power in a blast.

In about 1590 George Evelyn obtained a licence to install and equip powder works at Long Ditton (Surrey) and at Leigh Place near Godstone (Surrey). Soon after he and his brothers were approved sole makers of gunpowder in southern England by the privy council, on condition that they delivered a certain quantity of 'good and serviceable corned powder' annually into the royal stores. Their *quasi* private enterprise made the brothers prominent in the gunpowder world and their mills of prime importance. So the notion that gunpowder was a commodity in tight government control and that they had a monopoly of its sale and distribution is untrue. Despite the fact that the records of the stores of it are missing and that one of Lord Monteagle's relations by marriage evidently had charge of a store of it, some writers on the plot have convinced themselves (if not others) that Catesby and company could only have obtained gunpowder with the active connivance of the government. One Matthew Batty mentioned that Monteagle himself had purchased some, and in a copy of a note made by Sir Edward Coke, the price of the gunpowder discovered on 4/5 November was put down at £200. So how much gunpowder did this buy? The best figure from unfortunately varying estimates may be that of Coke himself who always said thirty-six barrels. Salisbury in writing to English ambassadors abroad described the amount as 'two hogshead and 32 small barrels' – which could be the same net weight. Recently a leading explosives expert, Dr Sidney Alford, has calculated that the plotters had something approaching 2,500 kg of gunpowder, which he has also suggested was five times the amount necessary to demolish the building, despite the fact that early seventeenth-century gunpowder was perhaps half as powerful as that manufactured today.[4] A reading of the Ordnance records by N.A. Rogers says that 18 cwt was removed from the Tower on 7 November.

Once in their new (and it was hoped) final resting-place, the casks were covered with firewood, 500 faggots and 3,000 billets, presumably carted in and then unloaded by hired porters. The material was piled over the explosive by Fawkes who now had time for such things, the mining having been ended to all-round relief. In Thomas Winter's confession of 23 November 1605 (regarded by Catholic historians as a fake, but now reinstated as genuine), he declared that the barrels were completely hidden so 'we might have the house free, to suffer anyone to enter that would'. Some writers have strangely taken this to mean that anyone could wander in from the street to saunter past the great pile in the underpassage. So how many people would want to go in there and where would they be going? The plotters had been desperate to hire the space because they knew no one paid it any attention – the former kitchen of the palace held no interest for anyone except themselves. Winter obviously meant by 'the house' the first premises rented from Whynniard wherein they had spent so much time in grubby and ultimately pointless labour. The plotters may have been too insouciant for their own good, but they were not fools, and they were not hankering to be captured through boldly parading their intent.

Barrels stacked, they thought their best option was to withdraw from London and Guy Fawkes went back to Flanders. Parliament was prorogued until

This extract is from the copy prepared by Levinus Munk, secretary to Salisbury, while the Hatfield draft manuscript, corrected by Winter himself, was evidently written on the earl's persuasion

3 October, and a plague-city like London while offering diversions was not a comfortable place to be. Thomas Percy kept the key to what had become an explosives warehouse that had to shift for itself. Amongst other places Percy went to Bath to take the waters in company with Catesby. This was intended as a physical restorative, but less easily repaired were his current finances since he was fast being pauperized by his own plot. Percy may expansively have promised to underpin all the expenditure by peeling off monies from Northumberland's rents, but so far he had done nothing to redeem his commitment. So Catesby very urgently needed to find new funds, and this meant risking approaches to men outside the currently tight posse of mostly inter-related plotters. It made for difficulties, as he knew from some uneasy resistance to the matter put up by his own long-serving retainer, Thomas Bates, who lived with his wife Martha and their children in a cottage on the Ashby estate. He had the distinction of being the only one of the core group who protested against the matter.[5] Before Catesby wooed and cajoled him into taking the oath, Bates had been suspicious and subdued, but when he took it and was charged with what it meant this became distressed agitation; and so troubled was his mood that Catesby sent him to confess to the trusted Father Greenway (Tesimond). Bates was to declare that the Jesuit had hushed his scruples by telling him of the merits of the deed, and bidding him be faithful and secret. Catesby was satisfied that his servant would not now betray him in any mode, but he foresaw still possible difficulties with others and he determined to obtain what he called 'the resolution of the Case' from his friend Father Garnet.

The Provincial of the English Jesuits went about unmolested and Catesby had no difficulty in finding where he was and arranging for a private interview on a question of conscience. Not that Catesby's own atrophied conscience had suddenly flared into action. Poor Henry Garnet was to be simply a pawn to be manoeuvred by a thoroughly unscrupulous man who went from Lambeth by boat, probably at night on 8 June 1605, to meet Garnet secretly at a house in Thames Street. The Jesuit liked a glass of good wine whether in company or not, and since Catesby said he was not consulting his friend 'sub sigillo confessionis', it seems likely that they had supper together, with Catesby informally soliciting an opinion. 'To his fast friend he opened up the Case as far as it was fit and the other willing to know it.' What Catesby did was fashion a careless curiosity as the talk moved towards the moment for the declaration of the critical question. In the quiet house 'on Saturday after the Octave of Corpus Christi' he rolled into the exchanges 'whether for the good and promotion of the Catholic Cause, the necessity of time and occasion so requiring, it be lawful or not, amongst many Nocents, to destroy and take away some Innocents also.' Garnet's later declaration, 'In truth I never imagined anything of the King's Majesty nor of any particular and thought it an idle question' sounds altogether too naive for such a man. It has a hollow ring today and must have seemed even more dubious to his interlocutors. To temper what may seem too harsh a judgment of the Jesuit, it can be said for him that as Catesby's preliminaries had been to do with war the question may not have seemed glaringly out of place, especially since it had been suggested that Catesby might be going to the Spanish Netherlands to be lieutenant-colonel in a new regiment. Garnet's reply was more transparent than the question: 'That if the advantages were greater on the side of the Catholics, by the destruction of the Innocents with the Nocents, than by the preservation of both it was doubtless lawful.' Catesby still pretended to have doubts, and after a glass or two of wine Garnet was quite willing to reel off his favourite piece of casuistry: 'That if, at the taking of a town possessed by the enemy there happened to be some friends, they must undergo the fortunes of war, and the general and common destruction of the enemy.' There was the most compelling statement yet and having given Catesby what he wanted by allowing his tongue to be uncurbed, Garnet suddenly became very frightened. Catesby agreed, of course, 'that he would never be known to have asked me any such question as long as he lived.' The disconcerted Jesuit stared at Catesby who pressed his hand in affirming friendship, called his servant and left. Garnet we learn now 'began to muse what this should mean and fearing he should intend the death of some great person . . . I would admonish him. This I did after at the house in Essex.'[6]

This second meeting took place in July at Fremland. Catesby arrived with Lord Monteagle and his cousin Francis Tresham. Walking in the long gallery, with Monteagle standing apart, Garnet said to Catesby that 'I wished him to look what he did if he intended anything. That he must first look to the lawfulness of the act itself, and then he must not have so little regard of Innocents that he spare not friends and necessary persons for the Commonwealth.' Catesby offered to get leave from a third party (Thomas Winter?) to tell Garnet his plans, but the latter

Henry Garnet, the well meaning, troubled Jesuit who took comfort in wine, was too Romanized to succeed in diverting Robert Catesby from disaster

declared himself forbidden by papal directive to listen. 'I told him what charge we all had of quietness and to procure the like in others.' This did not sit well with an exasperated Catesby: 'Oh, let me alone for that. Don't you see how I seek to enter the familiarity with this lord?' And so saying he moved off to talk to Monteagle. When Garnet felt bold enough to ask Monteagle himself 'if Catholics were able to make their part good by arms against the King?' he got a vague reply that James was generally 'odious to all sorts'. That Garnet had to ask such a question does suggest that he was being marginalized and worse (from his point of view) was to come. As for Catesby, he had evidently been aggrieved by what he considered the priest's unnecessary shufflings, especially since he was bound to have the 'resolution of the Case' as a sound prop when he approached at last those he had singled out to join the plot.

Soon after the exchange Father Greenway (Tesimond), confessor to Catesby, Winter and probably all the first seven plotters, rode to Fremland. He sought out Garnet in his secret room and begged him to hear him 'not in confession' but by way of such. Even an informal communication was horribly unacceptable to Garnet because being a shrewder man than he was sometimes prepared to admit, he had evidently guessed that Greenway knew Catesby's secrets. He told his fellow priest to keep his penitent's secrets to himself. This Greenway, now thoroughly agitated, declined to do and he entreated the shrinking Garnet to listen since the matter might injure the faith. The beseeching and cross arguing went on so long that Garnet, tiring of Greenway's importunings, suggested listening to his confession. This Greenway declined saying it was not his own fault that needed airing, and at length he prevailed on Garnet to hear him out since his risk would be no greater. Perhaps at this point, rather reduced by the argument, Garnet allowed himself a fitful hope that the matter would not chime with his worst fears, so having wrung a reluctant consent from his superior, Greenway told him of the plot.

It is possible to accept that the full realization of what was going on led to Garnet being shocked and distressed at the wickedness set before him. He believed it invited a common ruin and was a direct danger to him and Greenway. 'The Pope', he wailed, 'will send me to the galleys.' In contrast to this extravagant hand-wringing, Greenway coolly agreed that the danger was great and that an urgent appeal to the Pope was the only answer. At length the two Jesuits further decided that Catesby should be told by his confessor that Garnet forbade the design which was certain to draw condemnation from Rome. Greenway could also draw Catesby's attention to the muzzle on Garnet who became guilty of the crime of misprision of treason unless he broke the seal of confession. Of course it is doubtful if Catesby cared a jot for what Garnet thought, having prized out of him already 'the resolution of the Case'. Snatches of conscience among the other plotters were easily quashed if they arose, and except for Robert Winter the others were in any case too deeply committed to be likely to fall into serious agitation. They seem too to have been dominated by Catesby whose presence and leadership enthralled them and those who joined later. He had energy and administrative ability, while Thomas Winter and Guy Fawkes had the callous temper of soldiers. It was while he was in the Spanish Netherlands that Fawkes told Hugh Owen about the plot, and Stanley would also have been let in on the secret if he had not been absent in Spain. Owen agreed to tell him, even though at this time the old soldier was hoping for a pardon to allow him to return to England. As a realist Owen reckoned that Stanley would not be filled with glee at the wrecking of his personal effort, but when it happened he would go to England to assist in the aftermath. It was not by such men that Catesby's conspiracy was threatened with discovery; the danger lay with late-comers and innocent friends.

Garnet's second conference with Greenway was probably also at Fremland, when he renewed his protests. During this interview he explained to his fellow-priest 'he hoped to persuade Mr Catesby, who was not a bad man.' Did Garnet truly believe this or was he trying an oblique approach to secure Greenway's assistance? Certainly at this point he seems to have been a little more willing to hear Garnet's plain warning that it was their duty to inform their superiors in Rome, or to urge Catesby himself to submit the case of the English Catholics to the Pope to solicit his direction. Probably Greenway was afraid that stubbornness might push Garnet to declare the confession to be 'a Reserved Case' when only the Pope could decide what to do. Now he put it to Garnet that it would be sacrilege to break the Seal, but in the interim he would speak further to Catesby, who had a third interview with Garnet at White Webbs, Enfield around 24 July 1605. It was a favourite rendezvous where the Jesuits met twice yearly to confess and renew their vows in a very discreet half-timbered house full of trap-doors and secret passageways. Hidden among trees and not visible from the Barnet Road, it was rented by the third daughter of Lord Vaux, Mistress Anne Vaux, herself bound by the Jesuit vow of obedience. She was related to Catesby and was a distant cousin of sorts to most of the related plotters. She was also very wealthy and so endlessly hospitable to all Jesuits and secular priests who were called 'journeymen and workmen' by their friends.[7] As many as fourteen Jesuits at a time sometimes slept at White Webbs, two beds to a room – a ratio better than many inns. Anne Vaux was wont to assume the style 'Mrs Perkins' and to pose as the sister of Father Garnet (called Mr Meaze). In another persona she pretended to be a widow and it was as such that she was known to her servants. Gentle and very devout she did have some influence with Catesby and Garnet probably intended her to help him (at least indirectly) to frustrate what he called 'unlawful and a most horrible thing'.

Although Garnet's account shimmers with a deliberate vagueness, it is possible even so to form an outline of the conference between the two Jesuits and Robert Catesby. It was the latter's habit to stop at White Webbs whenever he passed through Barnet, and he was seldom long away because he had a great affection for Anne. On this occasion, to his great relief, Garnet had just received a letter from Father Robert Persons and this was presented to Catesby with a simultaneous admonition on papal policy. Garnet claimed that whatever device Catesby had in his head it would not prosper if it defied the will of the Pope. Catesby said that if the Pope knew what was intended he would not hinder it since it was for the general good of the country, and the more he was pressed by Garnet the more stubbornly he resisted, declaring that he would not listen to the Pope's will through a third party. Garnet then acknowledged the limits of his own credit with Catesby and read to him from the Persons' letter – 'a man everywhere respected for his wisdom and virtue' – pressing Catesby to acquaint the Pope with any scheme before attempting it. Catesby firmly declined to do so for fear of discovery. This duel of will and wits between allies eventually ended – the stalemate observed by the silent and deeply concerned Greenway.

What can be teased out of these reported exchanges nearly four hundred years later? Firstly, that Catesby's replies were careful and somewhat studied. Secondly, that Garnet's urgency, together with his warnings to Greenway and his messages by him to Catesby, meant that the Jesuit Provincial knew the secret heart of the matter. The seal of confession forbade him to communicate this otherwise than to Greenway himself. So in reply to Persons, Father General in Rome, Garnet fudged by referring in very general terms to the danger of private treason or violence against the king, and he asked for papal directives as to what was to be done in that case. 'I remained in the greatest perplexity that ever I was in my life, and could not sleep at nights . . . I prayed that God would dispose of all for the best and find the best means that were pleasing to Him to prevent so great a mischief.' Words that are poignant and ironic when we consider the fate of the plotters and Garnet himself. He had slid into a terrible predicament and no doubt he was sincere in his acute distress. But years of clandestine ministry against a background of persecution had led him to countenance treasons and plots against his country and his conscience was no longer as focused and active as it might have been. Indeed, it seems his sympathy was now more stirred by the recusancy fines and more minor hardships borne by Catesby and his cluster, than by the shocking fact that they were set to murder possibly hundreds of their contemporaries, including those who happened to live in the various buildings adjacent to the House of Lords. Garnet knew all this. If he had been a man of stronger character he must have been able to frustrate Catesby's plans for mayhem, and that without breaking his word as a priest. Garnet never identified such opportunities as arose because he lacked some of the finest moral constituents of courage. As he admitted: 'Partly upon hope of prevention, partly that I would not betray my friend, I did not reveal the general knowledge of Mr Catesby's intention which I had by him . . .'

The Jesuit came to rest his 'hope of prevention' on Catesby's reluctant consent to send an emissary to Rome to enquire further of the Pope's will. But Catesby made the requirement that the envoy chosen should also carry letters from Garnet, whose fear of consequences he had spotted. Under pressure Garnet weakly refused to do more than write to the papal nuncio in Brussels. Fear of the Pope made him try to shift responsibility. The lay envoy chosen by Catesby was his friend Sir Edmund Baynham, who readily consented, and may have had his own reasons for undertaking such a jaunt. As we have seen, he had achieved a certain notoriety that led to the courts and gaol.[8] So a somewhat curious choice, but Catesby evidently judged Baynham to be unscrupulous which suited his own plans. Catesby emphatically hinted that there would be something of a seditious sort attempted for Catholics when Parliament met, and he secretly instructed Baynham to delay his journey after he reached Brussels. He should wait for whatever might happen, then gallop to Rome to inform the new pontiff, Paul V. All this ran counter to what Garnet had wanted, and Baynham tarried in England until early September before departing with introductions from Monteagle to Catholics in the Spanish Netherlands and Rome.

SIX

Spies and Soundings

From about 1570 onwards the great men of the Elizabethan privy council were prepared to use spies to assist the making of policy. As a junior administrator in the 1580s and early 1590s Robert Cecil was able to give close scrutiny to the successes in this labyrinthine area, and during the late 1590s as he took on more responsibilities for implementing policy, observation became practice. Cecil showed an increasingly favourable attitude to the business of espionage and received many reports – some lame, some acute. All he lacked at this time to become a spy master to equal Sir Francis Walsingham (d. 1590) was a dark, even paranoid imagination.[1] Great vigilance was still required of the Secretary of State after the accession of James because enemies within and without did not generously melt away; the Bye plot and Main plot seemed to confirm this. But given the peace made with Spain (1604), much of the treaty being to England's advantage, Cecil might have been tempted to trim severely the intelligence cluster he had inherited from Burghley (d. 1598). Certainly a greater weight was now placed on career diplomats like Sir Thomas Edmondes in Brussels, Sir Thomas Parry in Paris and Ralph Winwood in the Hague, who conducted diplomatic business and supervised necessary intelligence gathering. But Cecil still used spies, and it has been averred that the government might have been more secure and knowledgeable early about the gunpowder plot if the Secretary had been willing to continue the previous employment of the ageing Thomas Phelippes.

Once chief of operations to Walsingham, he had evidently revelled in the arcana of espionage. Phelippes was a good linguist, with a particular gift for penetrating ciphers, and he had played an important part in the wrecking of the Babington plot, for which he received a royal pension of 100 marks a year.* When Walsingham died Phelippes allowed his skills and reservoir of knowledge to be bought by Essex, because the earl's political rival, Robert Cecil, did not like Phelippes, and he did not like Cecil. The reasons for this are now unfathomable, but perhaps there was an element of edgy competition between the two very short and physically unprepossessing men, with the hefty advantage of birth going to the hunchback Cecil rather than the pock-marked Phelippes. The latter evidently enjoyed money and eventually became Collector of Subsidy (Customs) for the

---

* John Donne characterized the skill of Phelippes as 'the art of decipherment and finding some treason in any intercepted letter'.

Dutch interest in the plot was high, and Sir Ralph Winwood, being close to Salisbury, could keep them informed as new aspects of the event came to be exposed

Port of London. This provided him with an agreeable house and a servant shared with his colleague Arthur Gregory, a Dorset man whose peculiar accomplishment (also valued) was to open sealed letters without hinting that a violation had taken place. The menage à trois was completed by Thomas Barnes, a spy employed by Cecil. Phelippes's port employment not only kept him comfortable, but also offered him the opportunity to follow ship movements along the estuary of the Thames, and to keep watch on any individuals who travelled abroad a little too often. One man with whom Phelippes had some contacts early in the seventeenth century was Henry Spiller (later knighted), an official of the Court of Exchequer in charge of recusancy fines, whose son was a suspect. Robert Spiller had been secretly denounced to Cecil, and it was noted that some of the family were known to be assisting Garnet and other priests in London; the young Spiller may have been a courier for Garnet.

In the spring of 1605 a spy claimed to have seen Robert Spiller in the company of Guy Fawkes, an event later reported by Edmondes. But simultaneously Spiller was somehow in London making friends with the household of the French ambassador, Comte de Beaumont, Christophe Harlay, himself an intimate of the Earl of Northumberland. Writing from Paris in March 1605 to Beaumont, Spiller said he had been ill and was going to convalesce in the country for two months. If the search for Catholic recusants in England abated he said he intended to visit

London for a short time after Easter. Spiller was well regarded at the court of the archdukes and meeting with de Tassis before the Spanish ambassador crossed to England, he was accompanied by Stanley, Hugh Owen and Father Baldwin. Such a huddle was suggestive to Phelippes who took it that some treasonable act was being worked up between London and Brussels. It was enough to set him off, warming to his favourite task of concocting a correspondence. So he began writing to Owen using the pseudonym 'Vincent', but Owen did not respond at all (which was also unusual) so in a flush of invention Phelippes amused himself by self-penning replies in cipher under the name 'Benson'. These he made pretence of deciphering as discoveries and he sent copies to Cecil. Unfortunately for him, Thomas Barnes had spotted the correspondence and snatched a letter from 'Vincent' to 'Benson'. The handwriting had such similarities with what Phelippes had sent that Cecil noted the fraud. Cecil had Sir Thomas Windebank arrest Phelippes, and he was required to deliver him to Cecil House without any exchanges with anyone on the way. One of the letters purloined by Barnes contained an innocent piece of gossip regarding Sir Thomas Parry intercepting a letter from Persons to Sir Anthony Standen (now imprisoned too). This made it appear that the luckless envoy was in league with Phelippes, and when interviewed by Cecil about what he was up to, all the cryptanalyst and forger could do was admit what he had done and excuse himself for an effort intended to make some money. Probably he would have been satisfied with a cut from the huge Spanish bribes that were then sloshing around the English court. Thoroughly peeved Cecil had him sent to the Gatehouse for meddling in state business, and later to the Tower where his visitors included Salisbury's own secretary, Levinus Munck and Sir William Waad. Had Phelippes been left to develop connections and then inform Salisbury, he might have traced back the connection between Thomas Winter's mission to the Spanish Netherlands in March 1604, the meeting with Guy Fawkes, and the arrival of the two men in England to meet Catesby at Lambeth in May. Phelippes probably knew more about the exiles and their business in the Spanish Netherlands than any secret agent then in the employ of Cecil. Periodically the Secretary could be too unyieldingly suspicious and Phelippes paid the price – in his case, despite the best efforts of friends like Waad, a lengthy period in the Tower.

But then neither side in the extended duel of spies could afford to be very trusting. There were double agents galore, including the Brussels-based Captain William Turner, a professional soldier with past service in Ireland, France and the Low Counties. Owen fell into the trap of employing Turner, who was already one of Cecil's spies, quite reliable over a number of years. Turner met Catholic exiles who told him to get in touch with Father Baldwin and Owen, and the agent first met the renegade Welshman when he was out walking with Charles Bailly. Owen's reception of the unknown soldier was not cordial, and several days later when they met again at the court of the archdukes it became evident that Owen had been doing some background research on Turner for he referred to his brother who was serving in the forces of Count Maurice of Nassau, asking if this brother could be won over to the archdukes 'and withal to render some town of importance'. Turner must certainly have been impressive under scrutiny because

Maurice of Nassau, a great soldier whose fame rests on the repulsion of the Spanish from 1590–1609. His grim childhood made him suspicious, resentful and unyielding

Owen gave him £100 and required him to go to Holland. Turner complied and when he got to meet Maurice told him of the offer concerning his own brother. Returning to Brussels with Dutch thanks and a reward in his pocket, Turner gave the exiles 'such things as I thought could best please their humours'.

In May 1605 Turner got to meet Guy Fawkes, out of England to avoid any government sweep. The two then went together to report to Marquis Ambrogio Spinola, the Spanish commander, on what Turner had done in Holland. Some weeks later Owen sent for Turner and they had a long conversation about advancing arrangements for an invasion of England, after Turner had been received into the Catholic Church by Baldwin. Since England and Spain had ceased hostilities following the treaty signed in London in 1604, and there was no exclusion zone around the English coast, a company of 1,500 Spanish troops were then in Dover awaiting passage to the Spanish Netherlands. The intention was to use them as a vanguard, reinforced by th volunteer regiment of exiles, as well as some three hundred English cavalry 'whicɩ he was assured would be ready to join them'. This must refer, even if the figure is optimistic, to the projected cavalry from the Midlands. From Dover it was envisaged the Spanish would move to Rochester where they would seize the strategic bridge over the Medway and immobilize the English fleet at anchor. Turner was himself told to wait in Dover for Father Greenway (Tesimond), who, returning with books and packets of letters, would then escort him to meet Catesby. According to Owen the plotters expected to use Turner in a freelance capacity, as the agent told Sir Thomas Edmondes. The ambassador was not impressed and for reasons of his own based on unknown evidence or maybe just intuition, decided that his informant was a feckless individual meriting little attention.[2] In a letter to Salisbury in late September 1605 Edmondes was most uncomplimentary, remarking on Turner's 'light and dissolute life' – an authentically stuffy English diplomat's cautious response. With Phelippes still in prison this attitude meant in effect that two vital conduits of information to Salisbury were blocked. Nor as yet did he receive anywhere near enough detailed material from diplomats like Parry who employed his own intelligencers. The lack of specificity extended for months and brought the government very close to having to dismantle the plot virtually as it happened. Their claim that it was the cryptic Monteagle letter which alerted them to the headlong progress of a projected calamity begins to look less unlikely, although candour was not a function of government, and Catholic historians have derided the notion.

Fawkes returned to England in September 1605 while Catesby was still grappling with the continuing problem of finance.[3] He had now sold Bushwood to Sir Edward Grevile in order to raise cash, but it cannot have been cheap to hire the ship of Henry Paris of Barking to take Fawkes over to Gravelines and then wait for weeks to bring him back in disguise with his companion. Besides, Percy had spent the others' money quite lavishly and even paid a man called York to do alterations on his hired premises. There had been a topping-up delivery of gunpowder to pay for, and because the plotters had grown more reckless their efforts had nearly been disclosed early in September by a servant of Whynniard. What John Shepherd saw was 'a boat lie close by the pale of Sir Thomas Parry's garden and men going to and fro the water through the back door that leadeth into Mr Percy's lodgings . . .' Thomas Winter later explained Catesby's hectic activity in town and country:

> Now by reason that the charge of maintaining us all so long together, besides the number of several houses which for several uses had been hired, and buying of powder, etc, had lain heavy on Mr Catesby alone to support, it was necessary for to call in some others to ease his charge, and to that end desired leave that he with Mr Percy and a third whom they should call might acquaint whom they thought fit and willing to the business, for many, said he, may be content that I should know who would not therefore that all the Company should know their names. To this we all agreed.

In Winter's testimony it was before Michaelmas that the meeting between Percy and Catesby, already mentioned, took place in Bath. Monteagle was expected to join them there, but there is no sign now that he did, although he wrote a rather swooning letter to Catesby as 'the dear Robin'. During their meeting Percy and Catesby talked about money and planned the rising in the Midlands. No doubt the latter heard reports of the very public private pilgrimage to St Winifred's Well, Holywell in Flintshire, organized by Father Garnet.[4] His interest in the Jesuit's effort would have been acute for in it Catholic wealth was on the move. In addition he might have noticed that Wales was stirring with sedition. From there the Bishop of St Asaph complained to Salisbury of 'the unfortunate and ungodly increase of Papists in my diocese who within the last three years are become near thrice as many.' A striking diminution of these numbers was achieved by Salisbury's agent, John Smith, an apostate Catholic released from prison in June 1605 on the promise of good service. Remarkably Smith delivered on this, for by mid-October the authorities locally noted with pleasure a huge falling away in recusancy. The rump that remained was for the most part comprised of women, and there were many of them too in Garnet's effort. No doubt he intended the pilgrimage to illustrate that the Jesuits still had some pull, but it is not inconceivable he hoped to get himself arrested sooner rather than later, hoping by imprisonment to escape the consequences of the dreadful secret vouchsafed him by Catesby. The news that Parliament was again prorogued from 3 October to 5 November seemed good, since delay might hinder the plot and give time for the anticipated interview between Baynham and the Pope.

Catesby's initial choice of keeping the plot as a family affair had been vindicated by the general level of secrecy maintained. But seepages about it there had been; how could the mouths of servants be completely stopped, or those of their wives? The uncertainty about the plot led to speculation about a coming

Young, rich and naive, Ambrose Rookwood was admitted late to the plot to fund it and supply horses from his great stable

'stir' during the next session of Parliament, but no one as yet could name the precise form. There was much expectancy and agitation among the leading Catholic families who eagerly threw open their houses to the pilgrims.[5] Indeed, the relatives of those same Catholic peers whose lives were threatened joined the Garnet excursion which started from Gothurst (or Gayhurst) in Buckinghamshire, the handsome property of Sir Everard Digby's wife. Their cover was a proposed otter hunt along the Ouse which flowed by the grounds. Digby was another cousin of Anne Vaux, and the house-party included her sister, Mrs Brookesby and her husband Bartholomew, whose death sentences for involvement in the Bye plot had been commuted; Ambrose Rookwood and his wife; Thomas Digby – Sir Everard's brother – and other leading papists. Besides Garnet the party included Father Strange,* Digby's chaplain, and that notorious lay brother (Garnet's server), Nicholas Owen (nicknamed 'Littlejohn' because he was so tall), a man much admired for his genius in contriving priests' holes. Altogether thirty persons started and rode by easy stages westward, being joined by others, and soon by Father Fisher. On the return journey they rested for a time at Huddington, the Worcestershire home of the Winter brothers, and also at Norbrook, the fortified home of John Grant. Salisbury did not attempt to disperse such a bold clan saying masses daily and passing through Shrewsbury with an ostentatious lack of discretion. When Holt had been reached a procession was formed, with the crucifix carried and led by the priests. The ladies of the party elected to walk barefoot the twenty miles to the shrine 'where all remained a whole night'.

Someone who reached Norbrook before the pilgrims was Catesby, welcomed by Grant, who took the oath of the plotters at this time and promised horses for the cause. Catesby left before the party arrived, probably to avoid Garnet, but he was anxious to intercept Ambrose Rookwood of Coldham Hall in Stanningfield (near Bury St Edmunds), Suffolk. Like Digby he was a young man (b. 1574) of privilege, head of an ancient and wealthy family, who had suffered like his neighbours and had been cited for recusancy in February at the London and Middlesex sessions, but was still affluent.[6] As a boy he had been educated by Jesuits at St Omer with his brothers Robert and Christopher who had become priests. Robert Rookwood was ordained in 1604 and had returned to England just recently – 'a little black fellow, very compt and gallant'. Catesby and Grant expected Ambrose Rookwood to ride ahead and probably the encounter was contrived by Thomas Winter to take place at Huddington, with Rookwood detached from his new bride, Elizabeth (née Tyrwhitt), the sister of Lady Ursula Babthorpe. What made Rookwood so ready to believe the well-rehearsed assurances of Catesby? Perhaps it was a residual naivety but there was clearly a great affection for an older friend 'whom he loved and respected as his own life'. Besides, Rookwood had often been in the convivial company at the Mermaid in Bread Street and lately both men had had adjacent lodgings in the Strand. Even so, at first the younger man baulked at 'taking away so much blood', for like other

---

* Arrested at the time of the plot, he was repeatedly examined in the Tower and held there until 1611.

conspirators he was liable to 'compunctious visitings of nature'. Catesby in his dominant mode was able to subdue such feelings in his friend by declaring that Catholic peers would be tricked out of attending Parliament, and besides, the priests had agreed to the lawful nature of the act. His Jesuit education having prepared the ground, Rookwood could not resist the seed.

Catesby's rides that autumn were all to a purpose. Accompanied as ever by Bates he rode on to Bedfordshire and stopped at Turvey for a meeting with Lord Mordaunt. But the visit was brief and later on Catesby spoke scornfully of him. Whatever the reason for quitting Turvey, Catesby was soon on his way to Harrowden (South Buckinghamshire) the seat of young Lord Vaux, because Sir Everard Digby of Stoke Dry, Rutland, one of the greatest landowners in the eastern Midlands, was now there and Catesby wanted to talk man to man before the ladies returned with Garnet. By every objective reckoning – he was married with two young children – Digby ought to have been beyond the most artful persuasion of the turbulent plotter. Especially so at this time because Lord Vaux, a boy of fourteen and the nephew of Anne, was just now betrothed. Digby's ward was marked out for marriage to the daughter of Thomas Howard, Earl of Suffolk, currently one of the most important figures of the Jacobean privy council. Catesby felt with a striking rush of tact that he could not immediately broach the plot to Digby at such a time; the juxtaposition of marriage and mass murder was too difficult even for him, but he stayed on at the house when entreated to do so. His presence was a shock to Garnet when within a few days the rest of the pilgrims returned, and Greenway must also have arrived separately since Bates later testified to seeing them 'all together with my master at my Lord Vaux's'. It was not a particularly comfortable house and somewhat dilapidated, so Digby in a buoyant mood invited the gathering to remove to Gothurst, a mere fifteen miles away, and he proposed that he and Catesby should ride ahead. The fine October morning gave the two renowned horsemen time to talk freely on dangerous topics out of hearing of all save perhaps Bates. Catesby was poised to reveal the plan.[7]

When they had gone some distance along the deserted road he told Digby that he had something important to say requiring an oath of the listener. Gentlemen of name and blood had been required to seal the oath with the sacrament, but Digby was known as so honourable a man that his simple corporal oath would suffice. Having flattered his companion (victim) Catesby drew his dagger and holding it out asked Digby if he would swear like the rest. Sir Everard agreed and repeated the oath of secrecy, expecting to hear of some attempt for the Catholic cause. Catesby then bluntly stated the whole matter and for a stomach-churning moment in silence Digby saw the true gap between reflection and intention. If he had not been seated on his horse it is not fanciful to suppose that his legs might have buckled with the buffet that took him to the edge. The anticipation of a fall into calamity made him fumble a response and he just managed to temporize when Catesby pressed for his consent and company in the project. As they approached Gothurst in silence Digby, who saw his comfortable future in brick and stone and glass before him if he did not deviate from the road before him, asked Catesby what would happen to their friends, the Catholic lords, if they took the other way. The reply had the authentic *froideur* of the enthralled fanatic.

But for his religion and the fixity of purpose it induced, Sir Everard Digby would very likely have become an ornament of the Jacobean court, lavishly rewarded for his fine bearing and good looks

'Assure yourself that such of the nobility as are worth saving shall be preserved and yet know not of the matter.'

Digby too may have longed to know nothing of the matter, and he asked if Catesby had placed it before Garnet or other Jesuits. Catesby affirmed that he had indeed and would not have acted without their approval. Seeing Digby's pained hesitation he then named the others in the plot, but his listener still felt he needed more time to consider such an extreme action. Feeling that Digby's full consent to join was of vital importance Catesby said that when they reached Gothurst he would show him the texts of their religion which allowed acts of violence against heretic princes. This seemed one way to head off a possible approach to Garnet in confession, since the Provincial seemed bound to contradict him and express his disapproval of the plot. Listening to the highly charged arguments for violence Digby began to doubt now his own particular hesitations and perturbations. In his initial reaction he had registered horror but its fullness began to ebb a little, for though in his private life he was a kind, moral and chivalrous man, he was also the type of religious sentimentalist who when his scruples were subdued could become unfeeling and cold-blooded. Besides 'his friendship and love to Mr Catesby prevailed'.[8]

When Catesby arrived back at his lodgings in the Strand for the beginning of Michaelmas term on 9 October, he gave a dinner at William Patrick's ordinary a few doors along. The guests were Lord Mordaunt, Sir Josceline Percy (a brother of the Earl of Northumberland), Francis Tresham, Thomas Winter, John Ashfield (married to Anne Winter), the playwright Ben Jonson and an unknown who may well have been the latter's close friend, Sir John Roe. A day or so after this Catesby and his associates rode off to Stratford, and their fortnight in the country was in part spent at Clopton by invitation of Ambrose Rookwood, who had moved there with his family because for strategic reasons his stable of quality horses had to be relocated to a position central to the plan. We know that Thomas Rookwood was there, as well as John Grant, one of the Winter brothers (possibly Robert) who helped Ned Bushell, also there, live impecuniously on an annuity of £50; one of the Wright brothers, Catesby and several more.[9] Strong agitation was now manifesting itself among the women linked to these men, and among women quite remote from the projectors. Anne Vaux, for example, went to Garnet to make clear that she feared some trouble or disorder and that other wives and friends had already asked her where they could retreat in safety until the 'burst' (uproar) was over with the opening of Parliament. They had taken their hint not so much from people as from the horses in numbers far beyond domestic requirements at Huddington and Norbrook. When Catesby had arrived at Harrowden just before he prevailed over Digby, he had soothed her agitation by showing her a letter of introduction from Garnet to a Jesuit in the Spanish Netherlands where he claimed he intended to go. First deal with certain home matters and then obtain an exit permit such as had been given to Thomas Throckmorton. Such a thing would be worth the £500 he was prepared to spend. Once away with his troop of three hundred horsemen he would enter the service of the archdukes since recruitment by them was legal since the peace of the previous year. It was a most useful piece of dissembling he used with others. Stephen Littleton of Holbeach House and his cousin Humphrey Littleton, brother of John Littleton, MP of Hagley House, convicted of treason in the Essex conspiracy, and who had died in prison in July 1601, were prominent figures in the Catholic community in the Midlands. Though friends of the Winters they were not thought suitable for the engineering of the plot, but Catesby while staying with Robert Winter did regale the Littletons with talk of his troop and suggested they might join it. Since Stephen Littleton was financially secure he was promised a command post and Catesby even offered to take one of Humphrey's illegitimate sons as his page. Then he invited them to the famous hunting party to meet at Dunchurch, where after sport he would tell them of the final plans for quitting the country.

Garnet meanwhile had Anne Vaux begging him to avert any mischief. He was aware of the signs himself, having observed Digby increase his stable of quality horses and Nicholas Owen start work on the device of a revolving floor into secret rooms and passages. With Catesby around both Garnet and Anne Vaux were uncomfortable at Gothurst, and as Digby arranged to rent the Throckmorton house at Coughton, Garnet promised to go there and celebrate Allhallowtide. Owen had worked there too but later demolition for alterations seems to have removed some of his handiwork. Probably Garnet had left Gothurst before the arrival of Guy Fawkes for whom Catesby had sent. The weather even pitched in to make things a little more troublesome with storms that tore at trees, rattled shutters and spooked horses. But the ride to Gothurst seemed essential, for Digby had promised £1,500 to support the plot after Thomas Percy had failed to pay the rent due at Michaelmas on the properties at Westminster. Fawkes was summoned therefore to take charge of any money and on his return to London, acting in his role as Percy's trusted servant John Johnson, he paid Henry Ferrers what was owed. He thought too about purchasing a topping-up supply of gunpowder, but there was another critical use for money. It was needed to hire the ship that would take him abroad after he had fired the powder train and ridden to Greenwich. He had been hired for his specific skills in blasting and was not required to take part in the rising that was intended.

Money, money, money! Still more was needed, Catesby knew it and the richest man known to the core of plotters was Francis Tresham of Rushton (Northants). His father, the very public Catholic Sir Thomas Tresham, proclaimer of the king's accession in his county, had died in September, leaving his son a rent roll of more than £3,000 a year at a time of heavily touted Catholic impoverishment. Sir Thomas probably died with some trepidation about his son, hitherto 'a wild unstayed man', now in his late thirties, whose mother had been a Throckmorton. Having fallen in with his cousins, Baynham and the Wright brothers in the Essex revolt, he had had to pay off court favourites to escape the wrath of the government. He had helped Christopher Wright go on his Spanish mission and had discussed armed revolt with his brother-in-law Monteagle, when they saw Garnet with Catesby at Fremland in July. Now married and conspicuously richer it seems very likely that his aggressive inclinations had been modified by the delightful bulk of his inheritance. Tresham's highly significant interview with Catesby took place on the afternoon of Monday 14 October at the Clerkenwell house of Lord Stourton, another brother-in-law. According to the account given later by Tresham he said: 'It would not be a means to advance our religion but to overthrow it, for the odiousness of the fact would be such as that would make the whole Kingdom to turn their fury upon such as were taken for Catholics, and not to spare man or woman so affected.' He developed then an interesting line of argument that if the then rulers of the kingdom were removed in such a cataclysmic act, the power remaining would fall into the hands of the Puritans and their ministers who would be supported by the Dutch.[10] 'The act seemed unto me to be very damnable.' Catesby bluntly made retort 'that the necessity of Catholics enforced them to try dangerous courses'. It was, of course, a necessity that had just been put on hold for Tresham. He tried another approach, endeavouring to persuade Catesby to defer until the end of the Parliament to see how Catholics fared under new laws. Go off to the Spanish Netherlands, he suggested, take your fellow plotters and take £100 to seal the matter. Yet in a perplexing addition he promised to give Catesby £2,000 at a later date, saying 'You know Robin that nothing but a bad cause can make me a coward.'

Meanwhile, there was a virtually simultaneous meeting of other plotters at the Bell Inn, Daventry, as the innkeeper, Matthew Young, later testified. Guy Fawkes arrived, having ridden from his rarely visited home county, and he ordered meals for a predicted group of six. Presently Thomas Winter arrived with one of his servants, and Bates and Kit Wright came from nearby Ashby St Legers. They expected John Wright as well, but when he failed to turn up Bates asked the innkeeper if there was anyone about to ride with a message to Lapworth. The commission fell to one William Rogers, the local blacksmith who did the outing by moonlight and returned with John Wright by seven o'clock the next morning. Thomas Winter immediately took him aside to show him an important letter he had just received (it must have been from Catesby) to inform him of Tresham's admittance to the plot – a step taken entirely on the initiative of the gentleman in red. There was a half-hour discussion before the group breakfasted together and departed.

The unsatisfactory induction of Tresham to the cause had led him to quit London at speed for his Northamptonshire home. At the great house there was a flurry of activity as within a few days he discharged his servants, hid family papers (which were not rediscovered until 1838), and shut up the house and required his mother and sisters to remove with him back to London. In company again with Catesby he seems to have reiterated that his support of the plot would be only financial. By now the sworn plotters were in, or making towards London, save for Thomas Percy and Digby who was selling cattle and sheep at Gothurst. Garnet and Anne Vaux were both at White Webbs for a few days, though the house had been more or less annexed by the conspirators and the atmosphere would have been tense. Probably both of them flinched for slightly different reasons when on 18 October Tresham (Anne's favourite cousin) turned up there for a meeting with Catesby, Thomas Winter and Fawkes. Then the most compelling question was how could Catholic peers be excluded from a massacre of their enemies. Uneasy that pity could still topple his plot, Catesby took a shrewd calculated risk in allowing a general discussion to develop because the simple notion of warning the especially favoured was deemed too loose. Thomas Percy naturally had a special care for the Earl of Northumberland, of whom there was some talk that he might be made Protector to conduct the government during a minority. Apparently it was Percy's task, following the explosion, to use his free access to court to kidnap the five-year-old Prince Charles. The Scottish nursemaid of the boy later gave written testimony that during October Percy showed a notable interest in her charge. Everyone was eager to warn young Thomas Howard, recently restored to his ancient title of Earl of Arundel. Catesby's contribution on him was to make the grotesque suggestion that the boy should receive a minor wound to keep him in his house and bed. Everyone was eager to save Lords Vaux and Montagu, and Tresham was vehement on behalf of his two brothers-in-law, Monteagle and Stourton. With Robert Keyes he spoke too on behalf of Lord Mordaunt which led a derisive Catesby to declare that 'he would not for the chamber full of diamonds acquaint him with the secret, for that he knew he could not keep it.' Besides, Mordaunt was expected to stay away out of choice rather than sit robed in the House of Lords while Protestant peers were with James at a service in Westminster Abbey. Catesby's bold and brutal rider to all this was that 'the innocent must perish with the guilty, sooner than ruin the chances of success'.

On 23 October a clutch of conspirators again dined at the Irish Boy, and the following day an even larger gathering took place at the Mitre tavern in Bread

Street, which ran from West Cheapside south to the river. There a watchful and discreet customer eavesdropped on the conversation and reported after the destruction of the plot 'there met at dinner . . . the Lord Mordaunt [so the plot itself evidently did not figure in the talk], Sir Josceline Percy, Sir William Monson, Sir Mark Ive, Mr Robert Catesby, Dr Taylor belonging to the Archdukes' ambassador, Mr Pickering, esq of Northants, Mr Hakluyt, and Spero Pettingar.' The reason the government was concentrating its attention on watching those in touch with the archdukes, was that it was hoping to learn something about the proposed English troop of Catesby and Sir Charles Percy.[11] Writing to Sir Thomas Lake who was with the king at Royston, Salisbury wrote in a confident mood: 'let his Majesty know that I dare boldly say no shower nor storm shall mar our harvest, except it should come from the middle region.' The last phrase could very well refer to the Spanish Netherlands rather than the English Midlands because the Secretary intended to make service with the archdukes virtually synonymous with treason.

SEVEN

Treason's Discovery

The cryptic letter to William Parker, Lord Monteagle, can be seen in two ways today just as it was when it was penned. First, that it was a genuine effort by a writer deeply concerned for Monteagle's safety to prevent his lordship's untimely death. Second, that it was a ruse of some sort to help deconstruct a plot that a watchful government suspected was underway, but about which it had too few details. Whichever view is taken, and there may be one or two delicate variations of both, it will be useful to sketch the character and career of the man who received it. Monteagle was the eldest son of Edward Parker, tenth Baron Morley and possessed a solidly Catholic background. His paternal grandfather had gone abroad in the late 1560s to join English Catholic exiles. His mother was a Stanley, daughter and heiress of the third Baron Monteagle, and it was from her he held his title; his wife was Elizabeth Tresham. With a cluster of friends Monteagle had been at the infamous performance of *Richard II*, in early February 1601 given as a clumsy curtain-raiser to the Essex revolt. Like Catesby and his brother-in-law Francis Tresham, he had been lucky to escape with a fine, but unlike the former he did not remain fired up with anger, although he was under house arrest at Bethnal Green and restrictions on his movements banned him from entering London for a time.

At length he had moved back into some degree of favour and had been among the group of gentlemen who had secured the Tower for the newly proclaimed king. In his employ as a secretary was Thomas Winter, so Monteagle heard the views of opposition even if he remained aloof by choice. He retreated from confessional politics and set about rebuilding his personal circumstances by dutiful effort. Hence Catesby had excluded him from the plot in all stages, though Monteagle declared his great personal esteem for its leader whom he held 'the only sun that must ripen our harvest'. For a time he reflected on the possibilities of service with the archdukes, like his friend Sir Charles Percy. But by 1605 Monteagle was sufficiently favoured at court to be selected as one of the commissioners for the prorogation of 3 October – very much a mark of distinction. Even Salisbury felt a greater confidence in him now and earlier in the year had supported him in a lawsuit against the Earl of Hertford. A few weeks before the delivery of the letter James personally asked Henri IV for the release of Monteagle's brother from prison in Calais, a request granted only with real reluctance. So Monteagle was slowly consolidating at last a comfortable insider's place in Jacobean society, although he had not entirely thrown over his residual contacts with the plotters. This meant he mingled with them easily and they may

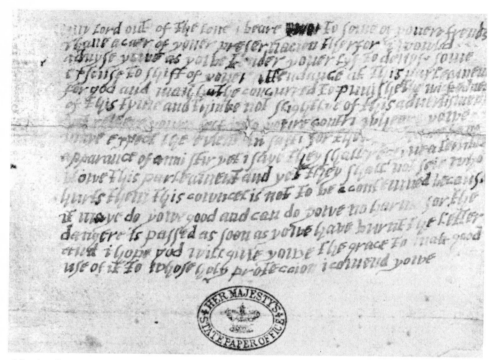

My lord out of the love i beare to some of youere frends i have a caer of youer preseruacion therfor i would advyse yowe as yowe tender youer lyf to devys some excuse to shift of youer attendance at this parleament for god and man hath concurred to punishe the wickednes of this tyme and think not slightlye of this advertisment but retyre youre self into youre contri wheare yowe may expect the event in safti for thowghe theare be no apparence of anni stir yet i saye they shall receyve a terrible blowe this parleament and yet they shall not seie who hurts them this cowncel is not to be contemned because it maye do yowe good and can do yowe no harme for the dangere is passed as soon as yowe have burnt the letter and i hope god will give yowe the grace to mak good use of it to whose holy proteccion i comend yowe

Ever controversial, the Monteagle letter is written in a hand unlike any other at that time. So if Francis Tresham disguised his own hand to pen it, how did he acquire paper evidently made in the Spanish Netherlands, where the government had many agents?

have individually or collectively been unguarded in his company. So there is at least a possibility that Monteagle revealed the story of the plot (as it was known to him) to the government before the despatch of the infamous letter. Whatever the case he was applauded and rewarded by a grateful king and government.

Conspiracy theorists over the years have battled over the anonymity of the letter and many names have been attached to it with varying levels of plausibility or implausibility. Some years ago in a previous book I suggested that Thomas

'The powder plot' was number seventeen – perhaps nineteen – in the long history of attempts to remove the reigning monarch between 1583 and 1606. The bulk of Catholics abhorred the idea of violence against Elizabeth and James. At this point only God sees the evil; his intervention is a sudden and dramatic reversal of the conspiracy

Phelippes had been put to write it for Salisbury, the most powerful man in the government, since he needed urgently to curry favour with him.[1] I do not think it besmirches the name of Salisbury to bend in the direction of the view that late in the day he understood the ramifications of the evidence of plotting and was desperate to head it off by some contrivance. Directing it to Monteagle with his many Catholic contacts and links to the plotters was a generous act and yet characteristic of Salisbury's pleasure in secret dealings too. In fact the contents of the letter are much less important than the letter as artefact – it was an attention-seeking object that allowed (encouraged) Monteagle to present it to the government in a very public manner. Moreover, since it was a gem of allusion and did not name anyone, Monteagle could present it without risking too much Catholic opprobrium. Indeed, he was praised by loyal Catholics or sometime Catholics like Ben Jonson, who wrote a verse encomium. Two further minor points lend some weight to the view that the letter was a government plant. On 9 November in drafting a letter to English ambassadors, Salisbury let slip that the

Monteagle letter had been 'in a hand disguised'. A Catholic historian, Father Francis Edwards declares that he could only know this if he penned the letter himself.[2] Secondly, the letter was written on paper from the Spanish Netherlands where both Salisbury and Thomas Phelippes had many active contacts. Given Salisbury's generally acknowledged subtlety in such matters it seems likely that he would have devolved the task of writing the letter to the most gifted man in the field of forgery. Or, as Mark Nicholls observed, the obviousness of the disguising may be meant to plant the thought that no one then could penetrate to the true identity of the writer; so don't bother.

Catholic historians and writers into the twentieth century have often presented the view that not only was the Monteagle letter a government device, but Salisbury himself was the arch-contriver of the entire plot and he somehow inveigled Catesby into it. Hilaire Belloc wrote 'we have evidence that he was secretly received by Cecil, and we are justified in suspecting, but not in affirming, Cecil's use of him; he could be used, as imperilled adventurers and double-dealing men often are by those in power, as an agent.' Well, yes he could, but is it likely? Dates become a problem here, because as Belloc himself noted the first date on which a conspiracy was alluded to in any surviving document as being surveyed by the government was April 1604 when Joseph Davi(e)s, a 'discoverer', contacted his superior Henry Wright, a part-time alchemist, who then wrote reporting the matter to Sir Thomas Challoner, a governor of Prince Henry with a line of access to Cecil. Nearly two years later Wright applied directly to Salisbury for a reward on account of his services 'in discovering villanous practices' which indicates that those he had been stalking had been exposed. More explicit still was a memorial presented later to James which was entitled 'Touching Wright and his services performed in the damnable plot of the Powder treason'. The king was reminded in that that Challoner and Chief Justice Popham had a hand in the discovery of the plot which they had periodically communicated to his Majesty. The point about the dates is that in 1604 Cecil had an extra burden in carrying forward the treaty negotiations with Spain, when he led the British negotiating team at the Somerset House Conference, and he had too that year responsibility for the Anglo-Scottish commission on union. This last could have been a woefully ill-sorted non-event; that it was successfully completed was in no small part the result of Cecil's careful working of the meetings. Would a heavily committed Secretary of State in his right mind also have set in motion a plot with a firebrand like Catesby to lead it? Viewed objectively (as far as possible) and in context, the idea is so bizarre that it is evident the proposers are frantically set on creating a black legend, with Salisbury set to emulate his Russian contemporary Czar Ivan IV (Grozny), whose furious, paranoid disposition came to rely on spies and terror.

Salisbury (he had become an earl in May 1605, so his elevation was not contingent on the 'discovery' of the plot) had come across plenty of froth about such things in his public career of over two decades. The challenge was to respond in a measured way, without instigating a reverse St Bartholomew's massacre; French Catholics were forever accursed in English eyes on account of that dreadful frenzy of public killings.[3] It was going to be, as Salisbury wisely anticipated, an extremely delicate matter to keep English horror and consternation within bounds once the plot was revealed. His own response to the letter was of course measured since it did not need to be anything else. All the sheriffs of counties who were due to relinquish their office on 5 November stayed on until the following January – another indication that by the end of October 1605 the government had arrived at a broad understanding of the purpose of the plot even if many details remained to be investigated. The letter was available from late October to underscore the possibility of being a Catholic and a supporter of James – unless, that is, your politics were Jesuit-inspired. The catastrophe of civil wars based on religion were difficult to ignore in their foreign manifestations, and neither James nor his chief minister had any intention of allowing such horror in Britain. This meant that the plot had to be seen as the work of fanatics of a peculiarly savage disposition, but all Catholics should not be tainted by it. It is even possible that by the mechanism of the Monteagle letter Salisbury hoped to save lives by jerking back the plotters to reality which they had left far behind for some fantastical realm of anarchic violence. Look! the government knows what you are about and if you stop now then you may save yourself as Monteagle has saved himself.

Indeed, Francis Tresham, most often declared to be the writer of the letter by those unwilling to consider Salisbury either cunning or benign, may have thought along the same lines. Catesby came to the view that Tresham was the culprit and he summoned him to an urgent meeting at White Webbs, along with Thomas Winter, who was told of the letter the day after it was delivered in such deliberate, one might almost say mannered, circumstances. Catesby and Winter were so incensed that the government had a line on them, and were so certain that Tresham had indirectly betrayed them that they seem to have decided *à deux* that if they could confirm their suspicions they would kill Tresham on the spot – one man, many men, it made no difference to them. So if Tresham had flinched or faltered a dagger or sword thrust had been envisaged. But having protested strongly against their intention to kill innocent people, Tresham summoned the inner strength to divert their wrath with a transparency of expression that held off his potential assassins. He was not the author; he denied it again by implication shortly before he did die a natural death in the Tower, but admitted then his past intention to reveal the plot to Sir Thomas Lake, one of the clerks of the council.[4] But then the reiterated denial may have been his last attempt to save his family from ruin. And if he had felt driven to warn Monteagle, why not Stourton as well, and why would he choose such a roundabout mode with its inevitable risks? A muttered warning could have done the deed. Perhaps it did since Stourton meant to absent himself from Parliament on 5 November. In this case, as in the death of Christopher Marlowe, it is wiser to choose the simpler option when trying to penetrate deep into the matter. The simpler option is again that the letter was manufactured by Salisbury to be sent to Monteagle to protect a source, and even bounce the plotters into action; the simplest that Tresham constantly lied. Moreover, something tangible like a letter was needed for James to ruminate over. Then he would have to conclude that there was a conspiracy against him (again), supported by a number of vehemently anti-Union activists. From about this point onwards Salisbury had a position of such superiority over

SERO, SED SERIO.

There was no one better placed by training or aptitude than Sir Robert Cecil to unravel the secrets of the plot. The notion that Salisbury fabricated the whole business for his own ends is false; a conspiratorial reading of history worked up by embarrassed Catholics

the plotters that whatever they decided – to advance or retreat – they were bound to fail ignominiously.

So, on Saturday 26 October, Monteagle was at his Hoxton house, once a Tresham property, for the first time in several weeks. He was eating dinner with company when outside an unknown man 'reasonable tall' (so at least Catholic historians cannot claim this was Salisbury), handed over a letter to a servant relieved of duties so that he could linger to take the air and watch the day dim fast. The letter was taken in to Monteagle at table and whether because as a well-schooled young man he had been taught not to read at table, or because his fingers were soiled with food, or because he had a shrewd inkling what was in it, having broken the seal he handed the letter unread (for all that it is short) to another servant requiring him to read it aloud. No doubt its roguish obscurities meant there was consternation at the table and Monteagle could then convincingly claim that it needed to be handed over immediately to the authorities. So he rode in the dark to Whitehall where coincidentally he came upon a quartet of earls about to take a late supper: Salisbury, Worcester, Northampton and Suffolk – men upon whom James primarily depended for advice about English matters – or, more accurately, 'to whom he entrusted English affairs while he hunted'. During the Essex revolt Monteagle had fallen into the Thames and nearly drowned; this time he unerringly found his way to the king's chief minister and his three Catholic companion-colleagues. The element of contrivance in all this is obvious.

The letter bearer sought to speak privately to Salisbury and this was a neat hook in itself, for Northampton was a man with a burning need to know everything having for so long been excluded in Elizabeth's time. Salisbury could therefore spread the burden of knowledge with due solemnity. The collective decision, no doubt made by Salisbury, was to wait for James to return from hunting at Royston. The king was at Ware on 30 October and reached Whitehall on the following day. Salisbury now had the ticklish problem of presentation to a man who displayed physical courage when in the saddle in pursuit of game. To overstate the threat laid himself open to rebuke as James chafed at the prospect; to underplay it was to miss out on the chance of consolidating policy. In the art of political presentation Salisbury was generally masterly and so the story was rejigged for recipients of state correspondence. Hence the modest differences between the account published in the *King's Book*, the account sent to ambassadors and the Lord Deputy on Ireland; and that sent to Henri IV, whose ambassador Beaumont was implicated or supposed to be implicated. There is no certain evidence of his guilt, but he quit England very dramatically and aroused suspicion even in France, for Henri declined to receive him.

When Salisbury got the Monteagle letter (back) from its recipient, he complained to his colleagues that he had been warning the king of a papist plot 'any time these three months'. Thomas Howard, Earl of Suffolk, who was lord chamberlain and had responsibility for the arrangements for the new session of Parliament reflected somewhat anxiously that the chamber was surrounded by houses and various rooms to which attention would now have to be paid. But it is symptomatic of the sometimes paralysing deference of ministers to their monarch that nothing was done until James arrived. It is very hard now, given the easy

A number of important figures in Jacobean England took issue with the king's view that for the sake of his health he had constantly to be in the saddle, recklessly charging after hapless game

larding of reports with compliments to James's courage and sagacity, to judge how immediately angry and shocked he was by the ugly news. As his solemn councillors stood in silence (or did they still kneel as before the late queen who had a haughty liking for such rituals), he read the letter and concluded as he had to that the intention was to exceed in violence the infamous explosion at Kirk o'Field in February 1567 when his own father had been a victim.[5] Did he ever reflect

The gallant *Eagle*, soaring vp on high :
Beares in his beake, *Treasons* discouery.
MOVNT, noble EAGLE, with thy happy prey,
And thy rich *Prize* to th' *King* with speed conuay.

Ben Jonson was another who praised Monteagle. Some years later Milton wrote a Latin narrative poem In Quintum Novembris, *a youthful interest that continued into old age*

on the uncomfortable affinity between the Stuarts and combustion? In fact, for a time he seems to have borne the prospect rather stoically as if he did not quite believe that the country which had welcomed him with joyous relief could harbour enemies of Scots and the union. John Selden, the English jurist and statesman, later wrote that the plot was generally supposed to be aimed against it.

Those about the king heaped praise on him for penetrating the mystery of the letter. Yet even in this it is possible to detect a thin and deeply buried element of contempt. With their obsequious praise no doubt they soothed the perturbation of a pained king, but they boosted simultaneously his own rather exaggerated sense of self-worth and this probably made it more difficult than it would have been to curb his excesses in the next twenty years. Perhaps they took it to be an act of kindness on their part to offset the full horror of the proposed act of dark forces. James was the champion of Protestantism, destined to unite the British Isles and he believed quite genuinely in a league against him directly fomented by Satan.[6] The uncovering of the plot in the coming weeks was then extended into months of effort nationwide because of new uncertainties, and it ushered in a period when the last vestiges of the Elizabethan era were shunted aside or just withered in desuetude. For some few this meant a dismal coda to their lives; Ralegh, for example, remained in the Tower until his last South American exploit and eventual execution. The gunpowder plot did give James a most striking opportunity to build an unchallengeable popularity, but he proved too inflexible.

The government had a few days in which to prepare for the crisis so enigmatically alluded to in the Monteagle letter. The plotters were under even greater pressure despite the heartening absence of names in it. None of them could be certain they were not under scrutiny, and if so, when their freedom might be abruptly curtailed. It must have taken an enormous effort of will to remain a unified family cluster, especially when one of their number was suspected of treachery. Tresham had quit London but returned on 30 October to join Catesby, Percy, Rookwood and Winter. Catesby employed Rookwood 'for buying of necessities for him', and at dinner soothed his subaltern by saying optimistically that nothing had yet been discovered.[7] This was contradicted by the news reaching Thomas Winter, but as Rookwood's young servant later testified, his master stayed in a house belonging to a Mr More outside Temple Bar. There he shared a bed (nothing unusual) with 'a tall gent having a reddish beard' – another resemblance between Catesby (it was he) and the late Earl of Essex. As for Fawkes, the inscrutable Yorkshireman, he went along to Westminster to check on the deteriorating (but still combustible) gunpowder. He was resolved to stay, committed to the momentous task for which he had been hired. He considered the plot just out of reach of scrutiny, and there was no evidence of any tampering with the explosive heap to make him think otherwise. He was not a man to desert his post.

Nor, according to his own account, was Thomas Winter, who seems to have got the news that the king and his councillors were consulting on the Monteagle letter from one of his lordship's servants. On Sunday 3 November confirmation of this lowered the spirits of the plotters still further, and Winter went to meet Tresham that evening at the latter's house in Lincoln's Inn Walk. Tresham's demeanour was so tormented that Winter was now convinced that he had betrayed the plotters, and he said as much when they met later. Some of them now looked wistfully at the possibility of an instant retreat to the continent, but the reluctance to accept that Tresham had betrayed them led the excitable and robust Thomas Percy to fix their fate. He called on them to wait to see what would happen over the next two days, and reminded them of the ship at anchor on the Thames at their command. At the first proof positive of danger they could hasten on board and drop down the river out of reach. Put with such impassioned conviction these arguments prevailed, but with a modification. Fawkes was to maintain his watch on the gunpowder; Percy and Winter would supervise the other necessary actions in the city, but Catesby and John Wright, who had lately removed from Plowland, his ancestral home in Yorkshire, to Twigmore in Lincolnshire, were to hasten north to put Digby and those about him on standby. Catesby's planning was not as casual as has often been claimed, and the vast explosion was intended as the first galvanizing action in the greater scheme. On hearing it at some time between 7.00 am and 9.00 am the proclamation of kingship was to be read and all loyal Catholics were expected to unite and seize

Did the plotters look anything like this? There is no corroborating it. Yet in the hand gestures the artist has thoughtfully hinted at the vehemence of these men, and a conspiratorial huddle is effectively suggested, even if Robert Winter is wrongly given prominence in the group.

control. The desire was to continue the succession in its legitimate course, but with Prince Henry likely dead, this meant the five-year-old Prince Charles, or his sister Princess Elizabeth, then living at Combe Abbey in Warwickshire in the care of Lord Harington of Exton, or even their baby sister, the English born Princess Mary. S.R. Gardiner commented: 'With the advantage of having an infant sovereign in their hands, with a little money and a few horses, these sanguine dreamers fancied that they would have the whole of England at their feet.'[8] But their situation need not have been as risible as this; the plotters had wives to call upon to help nurture the baby and children; there was at the end no shortage of money, indeed, the plotters were riding around with large sums in gold; and they were extremely well provided with horses in the right places as it was later proved when they fled north. Still, they might have been challenged by Princess Elizabeth whose anger at what was planned shows her to have been a spirited child.

It has been noted already that many of those who had participated with ill-directed energy in the Essex revolt were involved again in this treason. It is just this aspect of continuation which persuades the Jesuit historian Francis Edwards to reject absolutely the authenticity of the second plot. But this time there was no strong evidence of a would-be Essex in the offing as the days of political meteors were over and it was both easy and essential to be on the right side. In fact there were just too many earls for any of that rank to soar to the perilous isolation of Essex and when a duke later in the reign did reach such heights he was assassinated, rather as if Jacobean theatre had reached bloodily into politics. Even so, in 1605 there were definite long-term suspicions circulating about Henry

Percy, Earl of Northumberland, who had been ill-regarded for some time. When Thomas Percy went to a supper with his distant relative at Syon House on Monday 4 November, a day of extreme anxiety for the plotters, as minute by minute slipped by without further discoveries, the unfortunate earl was rendered so suspect that he would never free himself from the abominable taint of powder. Suspicion, too, fell on his associate, the scientist of genius Thomas Hariot, who had been persuaded to cast King James's horoscope. This auspicious act led to the ransacking of his papers and a period of imprisonment, during which time the ailing man was questioned by Salisbury himself as to whether his employer was aiming at the throne. Despite testimony from a number of sources it was too hard for the government in the circumstances to believe that the time at table and thereafter had been devoted simply to convivial talk. According to Sir William Lower, the earl's stepson-in-law, Thomas Percy had prepared a discussion paper on the proposed union of England and Scotland, and given his vehement antipathy to all things Scottish no doubt his tone was not cordial. Also at the table were a Mr Fitzherbert and Edmund Whitelocke.[9] The latter was a shameless sponger in society well known for the breadth of his interests; his patrons, required to have deep pockets, included the Earls of Rutland and Northumberland. After the exposure of the plot Whitelocke was arrested for being in the wrong place at the wrong time, but after a long period in gaol he was released since the investigators found nothing against him. The Venetian ambassador, Nicolò Molin recorded the government's view after 5 November that 'it seems impossible that so vast a plot should have been hatched unless some great Lord was interested in it, and there is not the smallest indication against anyone except this nobleman. Percy is his relation and his intimate, and as late as Monday last is known to have been in long conversation with him.'[10]

On the afternoon of 4 November the Lord Chamberlain, Thomas Howard, Earl of Suffolk, went on a tour of inspection of the parliament buildings. He was accompanied by Monteagle, whose curiosity was high, and Whynniard, who must have felt a pinch of apprehension. After viewing the Lords' chamber they moved downstairs for a watchful stroll through the lower-floor lumber room. Isolated in one area and hence remarkable they came upon an uncommonly large pile of billets and faggots, which they walked around before spotting a loitering serving man. He was asked who claimed it and Guy Fawkes (it was he) replied that it was Thomas Percy's in whose employment he worked. The court investigators then moved away and if Monteagle queried the reply, then Whynniard would have been able to confirm Percy's options on space. When they had gone to report their findings Fawkes had to quit his post to find Percy who could at that very moment of near discovery have been close by in the house Henry Ferrers had rented from Whynniard. If Suffolk had been adequately briefed by Salisbury and James perhaps he too left a watcher in the afternoon's shadows. Coming up on a deadline and with Suffolk's findings to guide them, the king and his advisers decided to make a thorough search below stairs by pretending to hunt for hangings and other 'stuff' if they were outnumbered and such a bluff was required. This time a Westminster magistrate and gentleman of the privy chamber, Sir Thomas Knyvett, was to lead a strong and armed group. The future

Nicolò Molin, the Venetian ambassador, at the time of the plot was an assiduous, if sometimes naïve reporter to the Doge and Senate

Lord Knyvett of Escrick was the brother of the Countess of Suffolk and well known to Salisbury since as young men they had taken their seats in Parliament together some twenty years before. Using him was a sign too of the many links between the Secretary and the Howard family.

Just before midnight on 4 November, Guy Fawkes had occasion to open the door to the under room. Whatever caused this – the furious barking of dogs close by perhaps, or the sound of a sword scraping the outer wall – Knyvett took advantage of the moment to order his arrest, an action without witnesses other than the guard. As Fawkes was pinioned Knyvett advanced into the black space with a lantern and then probed the vast heap of kindling until he came upon the barrels of gunpowder. Having made this extraordinary discovery he ordered then a search of the silent prisoner upon whom was quickly found 'a watch, matches and touchwood'; an item that on examination (16 November) Fawkes said would have burned for fifteen minutes – the time he needed to get clear to safety. The suggestive juxtaposition of all these things sent Knyvett urgently into the vastnesses of Whitehall Palace to meet his superiors. Those members of the privy council who could be found in the building were alerted to prepare for an immediate meeting in the king's bedchamber, and it was there that Fawkes was brought before them for preliminary questioning at about four in the morning of 5 November.

In this simplified image Fawkes, booted and spurred, is shown at the door of the Painted Chamber – quite incorrectly

EIGHT

After Midnight

It soon proved impossible to withhold news of the discovery and arrest, and by five o'clock on Tuesday morning Thomas Winter was alerted by the younger of the Wright brothers. Winter sent him to the Essex Gate to glean what further information he could, which when Wright rehearsed it on his return seems to have amounted to no more than before. Winter then sent him off to Thomas Percy bidding him to leave London although he meant himself to stay 'and see the uttermost'. The situation was not yet clear so Winter now went to the Court Gates and found them heavily guarded so that no one could enter. From there he went briskly to Parliament and in the middle of King Street had an encounter with a guard who would not let him pass. Making his way back to the Duck in the Strand where he was staying, he overheard someone say 'There is a treason discovered, in which the King and the Lords should have been blown up', which confirmed in essence Wright's prediction that 'all was known'.[1] Winter must have had an unshakeable faith in the ability of Fawkes to resist interrogation because he remained in London far into the morning, concerning himself with the fate of his fellow-plotters. As it happened, his assessment was well judged because the interrogation proved to be a difficult one for the cluster of councillors about the king. Fawkes (using his alias of John Johnson) appeared quite self-possessed, calm in aspect and lucid, if gruff, in speech. There was no immediate revelatory babble from him; the martial spirit held for a precious few days and gave his confederates more than enough time to quit London. Perhaps he even hoped that they could successfully regroup in the Midlands to initiate the revolt there; associates of theirs on the spot did not remain idle over the days of the crisis.

On Sunday 3 November, Grafton Manor, near Bromsgrove, the seat of (Sir) John Talbot, saw assemble a large company of his kinsmen and friends. From Huddington, some nine miles away had come Robert Winter, whose reluctance months before to follow his own brother and Catesby has been noted. His companions now were Robert Acton and his two sons, and the quartet stayed the night at Grafton, before departing on the morning of 4 November with Talbot who probably left them at Bromsgrove to ride on to his other estate at Pepperhill, near Albrighton, in Shropshire.[2] Robert Winter's servants had brought along several remounts, horses just recently sent to Huddington by Sir Everard Digby, and the party now went on to Coventry where they spent the night at the Bull Inn in Smithford Street. Here they were joined by Winter's cousins, the Littletons, Stephen and Humphrey and together they left the town on the morning of

5 November to join the rendezvous at Dunsmore Heath, the party picking up more horsemen as they went. At Dunchurch Winter left the Littletons and rode on to Ashby St Legers, some six miles further east where it was expected that Catesby would call on his way from London. At about six o'clock when Winter had just sat down to supper with Lady Catesby, a messenger arrived for him. The man came with an urgent message from Catesby, who did not dare approach his mother with the truth and so was waiting for Winter just outside the village. Quitting London at about eleven he had ridden eighty miles in seven hours, the relays of horses being provided by Ambrose Rookwood, one of the last plotters to leave London. Having a superior mount he overtook Robert Keyes about three miles beyond Highgate and then picked up Catesby and John Wright beyond Brickhill. A little further on they came upon Thomas Percy and Kit Wright, and the little cluster of five now rode ensemble, Percy and John Wright dumping their cloaks in a hedge 'to ride the more speedily'. I doubt if the 'fair scarf' Rookwood had had made was tossed aside so unceremoniously since it may have had some sort of emblematic significance in the decoration of pattern. Writing at the end of the month Waad drew attention to these items: 'I perceive there were very fair scarves made for divers of them.' He was evidently impressed and a little envious that Rookwood had too a Hungarian-style horseman's coat 'lined all with velvet'; a beguiling image of a young man's vanity.[3] Still, I doubt that even he would have worn such an eye-catching item for a mud and sweat-lathered retreat.

A former intelligencer, Sir William Waad was made Lieutenant-Governor of the Tower of London in 1605, to the consternation of Ralegh

Catesby could hardly dissemble with Robert Winter in such a situation – 'Mr Fawkes was taken, and the whole Plot discovered.' Winter asked him what he meant to do, suggesting that all should throw themselves on the king's mercy 'and by God's grace, his Majesty would yield the least deservers some favour'. Catesby, of course, would have none of it and said he would ride to Dunchurch to consult. At the Lion they joined the company assembled which at first numbered about one hundred, but on hearing the desperate news some began to withdraw and by ten o'clock only about forty remained to concert measures for their escape.[4]

Among those who stayed was John Winter. He had spent Monday night with his brother-in-law John Grant at Norbrook, and the next day they had ridden on to Rugby where as they were preparing for bed in an inn a messenger from Dunchurch summoned them. After a hasty meal and a short rest the cavalcade left Dunchurch before eleven and travelled to Warwick where at about midnight they raided the stables at Warwick Castle and took nine or ten horses belonging to Mr Benock, leaving him their tired ones. The proceeding dismayed Robert Winter who told Catesby to desist since 'it would certainly make a great uproar in the country', and it would further blacken their reputations in the eyes of the king. Catesby's answer was a brisk 'some of us may not look back'. Robert Winter evidently hoped otherwise and said so, to which Catesby's sardonic response was: 'What, hast thou any hope, Robin? I assure thee there is none that knoweth of this action but shall perish.'[5] Fresh horses – a new destination – John Grant's house at Norbrook, about four miles away, near the village of Snitterfield. While there Digby wrote to his wife who was still at Coughton (near Alcester), a distance of about ten miles, so quite easily covered by Bates who was able to detail the story of the failure to her and the two Jesuits Garnet and Greenway. Then the large company of fugitives was on the move again, armed now with between fifty and sixty muskets and callivers and a good supply of powder and shot laid on by Grant. Their course was still westward and passing through Snitterfield they forded the Alne before reaching Alcester where they were joined by Greenway. Catesby greeted him warmly as a gentleman who would 'live and die' with them, a notion that proved quite incorrect because Greenway eventually managed to escape abroad. It was but a reminder of Catesby's bravado in the face of compelling evidence that fewer and fewer would be willing to sacrifice themselves for a lost cause.

Their route now probably took them through the village of Arrow and then along the Worcester road before shifting to the by-lanes to Huddington which they reached at about two o'clock on Wednesday afternoon in a state of exhaustion. Towards evening Thomas Winter arrived having ridden alone from London across country, and his brother John then set guards at the corners of the roads. The rest of the shrinking company (now down to about thirty) slept until three o'clock in the morning (Thursday 7 November) when they were roused by the women in the house to attend the Mass administered by Father Nicholas Hart, who heard their confessions. Then in the hall they helped themselves from arms, armour and ammunition laid out on long tables, before loading carts with the remainder. At about six on that chilly November morning the time came for the final parting, and they moved off intending to make for Wales where they

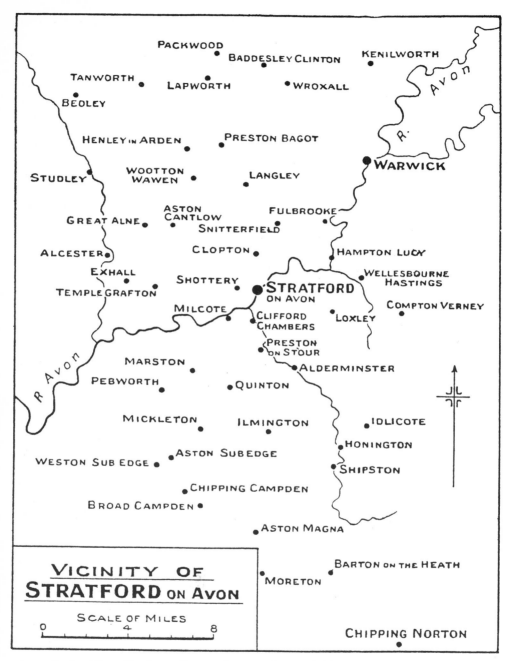

PACKWOOD
BADDESLEY CLINTON
KENILWORTH
TANWORTH
LAPWORTH
WROXALL
BEOLEY
HENLEY in ARDEN
PRESTON BAGOT
R. Avon
WOOTTON
WAWEN
LANGLEY
WARWICK
STUDLEY
ASTON
CANTLOW
FULBROOKE
GREAT ALNE
SNITTERFIELD
ALCESTER
CLOPTON
HAMPTON LUCY
EXHALL
SHOTTERY
WELLESBOURNE
HASTINGS
TEMPLE GRAFTON
STRATFORD
ON AVON
COMPTON VERNEY
MILCOTE
CLIFFORD
CHAMBERS
LOXLEY
R. Avon
PRESTON
on STOUR
MARSTON
ALDERMINSTER
PEBWORTH
QUINTON
MICKLETON
ILMINGTON
IDLICOTE
ASTON SUBEDGE
HONINGTON
WESTON SUB EDGE
SHIPSTON
CHIPPING CAMPDEN
BROAD CAMPDEN
ASTON MAGNA
BARTON on the HEATH
VICINITY OF
STRATFORD ON AVON
MORETON
SCALE OF MILES
0   4   8
CHIPPING NORTON

Across England from Humber to Severn, there stretched a solid belt of obstinate, moneyed Catholic squiredom. The cluster around Stratford on Avon and Warwick became especially important in the plot

hoped to receive assistance from their numerous Catholic friends. The gloom of the morning as they made their way to Hanbury and across Bentley Heath, seems to have matched that of the horsemen, because before they reached Hewell Grange, the Worcestershire home of Lord Windsor, Catesby had to box in the servants by having four of the principals at the head of the cavalcade, and four gentlemen at the rear (Thomas Percy, John Grant, Henry Morgan and one of the Wright brothers). At the Grange, according to a servant of Digby – William Handy – 'while some few sat on their horses to watch who should come into the house, the rest went into the said house, and broke into the armoury, took out the armour, and caused themselves all to arm themselves, and the rest of the armour they put into a cart, and carried away with them, and they also helped themselves to a supply of powder, and, finding a trunk containing from £1,000 or £1,200, they took away £60.' Such a large posse of horsemen drew in intrigued villagers in some numbers, but no one seems to have taken the opportunity for some looting and no one joined the insurgents.

They now took off with their plunder, going through Burcot, Lickey End, Catshill, Clent and Hagley to Stourbridge. Autumn rains had made the road exceedingly difficult, and the fording of the Stour, at a seasonal high, led to the unfortunate wetting of the gunpowder. Such conditions also provided opportunities for servants to desert and despite the efforts of the gentlemen the party was further diminished by the time it had reached Holbeach House, the home of Stephen Littleton, at about ten o'clock. It had taken them some sixteen hours to travel twenty-five miles, and they needed rest and food, as well as an opportunity to disuss their dismal situation. Not one Catholic had thought to join them and news arrived shortly that they were being trailed by Sir Richard Walsh, sheriff of Worcestershire. A general understanding seems to have been reached at this point that they needed to make preparations to resist an assault on the house. They were extravagantly well provided with weapons and armour but sorely lacking in numbers, so their thoughts turned to John Talbot, who as we know, was on his way to his Shropshire estate at Pepperhill which was ten miles from Holbeach. The obvious delegate to go to Pepperhill was Robert Winter, Talbot's son-in-law, but he refused saying that Talbot was certain to look after his daughter when she became a single parent. So it was Thomas Winter who volunteered to go, in company with Stephen Littleton, and long before dawn they were in the saddle again bound for Pepperhill. The house was situated on a high promontory of land with extensive views over the country, and Talbot had too a bowling green close to his door.[6]

At about eight o'clock on Friday morning, Talbot was out of the house going to the green when he spotted Winter approaching on foot. From his later testimony Talbot did not greet him at all warmly but baldly asked him what he was doing there. Winter replied: 'Why should I not come hither?' The next exchanges revealed why – Talbot wanted him off his property – 'I pray you get hence', to which Winter replied: 'If you like my company no better, God be with you.' Rebuffed, Winter and Littleton disconsolately retraced their journey back to Holbeach where news of a further calamity awaited them. Not only had Digby found an opportunity to flee, but the rest were in some disarray because having set some wet gunpowder on platters to dry before a fire, an ember had fallen onto one and caused an explosion. It was a pitiful replica on a small scale of what they had intended in London; Catesby and Rookwood were both badly burned, and it settled for Robert Winter and Stephen Littleton what they had to do in these dire circumstances. Both quit the house singly before subsequently meeting in an adjoining wood. A more purposeful Thomas Winter remained and he dressed the wounds of his friends as best he could before defining measures for the defence of the house. There was little to do and the sheriff's force surrounded the house around eleven, started a fire and stormed the building. In the mêlée Thomas Winter was shot in the shoulder; the Wright brothers were killed and Rookwood further wounded. Catesby, Thomas Percy and Thomas Winter stood close together in a defensive knot before the former two died (as it seemed to Winter, himself piked in the stomach) shot with one bullet. In a more lurid version of this climax to the plot, Catesby was shot outside but dragged himself inside to kiss a picture of the Virgin Mary, before dying with it in his arms. Purists will doubtless prefer the more austere first version, but most will flinch at the immediate plundering of the corpses. Kit Wright's boots were heaved off in order to secure his silk stockings, and someone certainly spotted the special swords of some of the gentlemen.* (See Appendix II.)

Of those who had just quit the house before the final assault, Digby was soon recaptured with two servants – possibly Thomas Bates and his son. The trio had taken horses and headed for the woods nearby where a dry declivity that they came across might have afforded them a temporary hiding place if their tracks had not been visible in the mud and leaf-mould. The cry went up that Digby had been found and he confirmed it with an abrupt 'Here he is indeed', edging his mount out and up trying to pass through the advance horsemen. Then he was confronted by a much larger cluster behind and he gave himself up. Those captured at Holbeach were then conveyed to London to the Tower, while John Winter, who seems to have escaped from Holbeach in the middle of the night, determined to throw himself upon the king's mercy. His brother Robert and Stephen Littleton, however, remained at large, and the government later in the month put out a description of the two fugitives.

'Robert Wynter [sic] is a man of meane stature rather low, than otherwise, square made, somewhat stooping, near forty years of age, his hair and beard browne, his beard not much, and his hair short.'

'Stephen Littleton is a very tall man, swarthy of complexion, of browne coloured haire, no beard, or little, about 30 years of age.'

Humphrey Littleton, who had returned home directly from the gathering at Dunchurch, bribed one of his tenant farmers near Rowley Regis to hide his cousin and Robert Winter for a time, and subsequently they moved from one farmhouse to another during the coldest time of the year, eking out the modest fare offered them. Early on New Year's Day (by our reckoning) they fetched up at

---

* Sir Thomas Lawley, who was with Walsh, reported to Salisbury that 'the rude people stripped the rest naked'.

Hagley, at the house of a family tenant – one Perkes. They gave him £30; his man £20 and his maid £17 as an earnest of their gratitude. Perkes put them in a barley-mow in his barn and they were given food and drink for the next nine days, concealed by winter straw piles. In the middle of the tenth night while they slept, a drunken poacher named Poynter took shelter in the barn and climbed onto the straw before lurching unexpectedly into their hollowed-out space. The two men seized him and with the aid of Perkes (to whom he was well known), the poacher was forcibly detained by them until the fifth day when he outwitted them and escaped. The news of this misfortune was taken to Humphrey Littleton at Hagley House and it was there that Perkes escorted the fugitives that night for the joy of food, drink, clean clothes and a bed. Such an effort in the house required compliant servants if it was to succeed for any time, and Littleton's cook was the one who promptly betrayed his employer and unhappy wanderers. Soon they were resting uncomfortably in the Tower.

The town and country sweep by the government's officials naturally extended to Francis Tresham's county of Northamptonshire, where the sheriff was Sir Arthur Throckmorton. He was in London when the high drama broke on 5 November and he went quickly off to his territory for a muster of loyalists. He summoned his fellow justices of the peace, Sir Richard Chetwode and Sir William Samwell to meet him at Rushton, and the Tresham mansion was searched under their supervision. Then the party moved on to Mordaunt's property at Drayton, and afterwards Throckmorton caught up with one of the unfortunate mothers, Lady Tresham, who had left London for Liveden. Throckmorton's penultimate stop was Ashby St Legers to seize Catesby's goods, and then came the rumpus at Harrowden, the home of Lord Vaux. Great hopes were entertained of finding Father John Gerard there and the house was investigated by at least three hundred men who pried and probed for two or three days while Anne Vaux and her young nephew vigorously denied all knowledge of the plot. As it happened, Gerard escaped and eventually crossed to Europe, while the pious lady of the house was taken to London for examination, as were many wives of conspirators.

The Tower of London became the hub of the investigation, but some preliminary work was done in the provinces with captives. On 8 November, still smarting from his wounds and burns, Ambrose Rookwood was taken before Sir Fulke Greville (snr), one of the great men of Warwickshire – Alcester became a family property. As Deputy Lieutenant of the county he had been alarmed by the raid on the stables in Warwick and he had roused the locality that something more than a robbery was afoot. Asked why he was abroad in the county Rookwood said he was going to Worcester to meet a man (one Ingram) who had sold him a hawk. When his servant William Johnson was asked the same question he recalled the hawk but got into a muddle about the town and said Hereford. Afterwards Greville wrote breezily to Salisbury that he hoped to be able to send him one of the horses left behind in the raid.[7] Rookwood was interrogated in the Tower but it soon became evident that this hapless young man had little significant knowledge of the inner workings of the plot. Digby, less naive, probably struck the interrogators as a more likely source of real details and he was examined on two successive days, 19 and 20 November at some length before the lords commissioners. Their problem for now was that so many violent, abrupt deaths had already happened their lines of enquiry about 'the most cruel and detestable practice . . . that ever was conceived by the heart of man' were severely reduced. Still, writing to the English ambassador to Spain, Sir Charles Cornwallis, Salisbury was both realistic and optimistic: 'It is also thought fit that some martial man should presently repair down to those countries where those Robin Hoods are assembled, to encourage the good and to terrify the bad . . . although I am easily persuaded that this faggot will be burnt to ashes before he shall be twenty miles on his way.' It was Cornwallis in high spirits who planned the first ever fireworks party to celebrate the failure but he called it off despite his initial impression that the Spanish king and court were shocked.

After 12 November (the day Tresham was arrested), the government's officials were preparing for the arrival of more prisoners and prisoners' wives. They were also making other arrests, such as those on 15 November of Lords Montagu and Mordaunt – neither of whom had intended to be in Parliament on the day. Northumberland was now quarantined in Lambeth Palace with Archbishop Bancroft, whose initial response to the discovery of the plot had been to panic, rushing to the safety of his residence to pen a hasty letter to Salisbury about a possible sighting of one of the conspirators. Evidence that unlike the Bye plot it was an exclusively Catholic effort, may have caused the archbishop a twinge of regret that no puritans had meddled. Even the dead were not overlooked, for a privy council order was sent to Staffordshire for the slain of Holbeach to be exhumed and quartered. By the time of the trials the heads of Catesby and Percy were 'upon the side of the Parliament House', and what was said to be Tresham's (dead of a strangury – a dysfunction of the urinary system leading to acute retention – while in the Tower) was fixed to London Bridge. Thus the hated and condemned became sightless spectators of their own failure. Such a macabre proceeding as quartering of bodies had a particular purpose identified approvingly by an anonymous pamphleteer in the Low Countries some years before this: 'The standing quarters in England show God's blessing upon that nation, who dothe reveal them, and the justice of the country that doth punish them.'[8] Deliverance from the plot in the view of Bishop Lancelot Andrewes was due to God alone and the English must recognize the intervention of their Saviour. In his first plot sermon the following year he did not hesitate to compare the deliverances of Britain within recent memory with the Passover of the Hebrews. Stern triumphalism was often the tone after the plot.[9]

One of the New Testament group at Westminster chosen to translate the Epistles for the so-called King James version of the Bible was Dr William Barlow. Dean of Chester and then Bishop of Rochester, with his mastery of language and rhetorical devices, he was a natural choice for the delivery of a Paul's Cross sermon. It was calculated to be a chilling effort, and while references to Fawkes as more evil than Caligula, as 'the devil of the vault' and 'Blood-sucker', suggest the bishop was over-excited, no doubt it had an effect on his listeners. Indeed, in *Macbeth* there is the same sulphurous tone with the appearance too of demonic forces. Fawkes at this time was still alive, albeit faltering as he was subjected to torture. The notion that this item in the government's armoury was dealt out indiscriminately is quite wrong, and they obtained a useful amount of (so to speak) leverage by using it with care. Salisbury was well aware that torture can induce a man to say anything and that was not what was wanted. So many of the conspirators were now known by the others to be in the Tower, and each was so much afraid of what the others might have confessed, that they spoke freely when examined. Each feared that at any moment the rack might be employed on him. The government meanwhile decided to use Fawkes for a propaganda programme by working up his confessions for publication. It gave them an opportunity to sneak in a reference to contacts between Fawkes and Owen in the hope and intention of ruining an enemy exile of many years. Salisbury wrote to Sir Thomas Edmondes on 14 November to declare that Owen had been definitely incriminated by Fawkes. Edmondes might have put this about with confidence in Brussels since the news came from his superior, but it was actually untrue, because according to the surviving evidence Fawkes did not mention Owen until 20 January 1606.

The assertion did, however, get some much needed backing by the confession on 23 November of Thomas Winter, who had like Rookwood survived his injuries. Catholic historians and apologists have constantly denied the authenticity of this confession because the manuscript version at Hatfield, an autograph example, has a variant signature substituting the unique spelling Winter for the usual form of Wintour which he used. No one has ever made a solid and sensible suggestion about why a government-employed forger (say Thomas Phelippes) would deliberately make such an error in a crucial state document, and why Salisbury would let it pass. Winter had an injured shoulder

This confession was taken by Coke, Waad and Edward Forsett for the lords commissioners. It was written by a clerk and signed by Fawkes at the foot of each page

Guido fawkes,

Guido fawkes

Guido

Fawkes's signature became progressively more wobbly as he was tortured in the Tower

and penning his name in a simpler form may have been easier. Whatever the reason for this tiny (albeit eye-catching) blemish, it was written without immediate duress and the text was incorporated into the portmanteau publication known as the *King's Book*. This was a highly coloured official account of the treason, printed at the end of November, and ready for circulation early in December.[10] For those outside the privileged cluster of councillors and courtiers it was powerful and essential reading just as the Secretary intended. It told enough about the plot to convince Londoners and direct their thinking on the matter. One reader hot to take it up seems to have been William Shakespeare and the little quarto set him to thinking about a Scottish play and the death of kings. When the conspirators were hauled to London the *King's Book* noted how the people wished to see them 'as the rarest sort of monsters; fools to laugh at them; women and children to wonder; all the common people to gaze –'. In *Macbeth* when Macduff has cornered the usurping king, he uses the same language as he taunts him:

> Then yield thee, coward,
> And live to be the show and gaze o' the time
> We'll have thee, as our rarer monsters are,
> Painted upon a pole (V. viii, 23–6)

The planned atrocity was widely regarded as so brutal in design and evil in its scope that a demonic element was certain; 'night's black agents' gave it a wild impetus. The association of evil with darkness is a very old notion 'but it became the universal thought of England in the winter of 1605–6'. Lancelot Andrewes: 'In darkness they delighted, dark vaults, dark cellars, and darkness fell upon them for it'. In many contemporary prints this 'foul and filthy air' is pierced dramatically by a shaft of light from Heaven. Satanic meddling was not invented by James for polemical purposes, nor for the gratification of massaging his own vibrant sense of self-importance. It was an opinion fully shared by the principal judges of the Scottish bench and by privy councillors.[11] It was a traditional view taken of earlier plotters like Bothwell and Gowrie, for James 'regarded himself and his like as capital objects of dispute between the forces of evil and of good'. A

A multiple image linking the Spanish Armada and the plot; the Papacy and the Jesuits are seen in conference with laymen and a demon. By yoking the conspiracy to hellish forces all commentators could arouse concern for the rest of the century

letter from the privy council of Scotland sent to James in November confirms their state of mind: 'Since the glad tidings came to us of your Majesty's happy delivery from the abominable conspiracy so inhumanly contrived by the devil and his supporters against your royal person, the Queen and your Majesty's children.' On 26 November there was a Proclamation to the Fencibles of Scotland to be prepared to defend James, and it contains the following: 'this detestable plot which without the concourse of all the devils and malignant spirits within the precinct of this universe, their supporters and deputies upon the face of the earth, could never have been excogitated.'

Despite the bristling sense of horror and terror – it was in a sense a grand succession crisis averted – and James in his twenty minutes 9 November speech to Parliament affirmed that 'these wretches thought to have blown up in a manner the whole world of this island', there was no pogrom aimed at the Catholic community. This is a fact that Catholic historians distressed by the ignoble purpose of Catesby and company always whizz over in silent disbelief. Restraits of law, albeit a little stretched, remained and James himself kept his head as far as the papist minority were concerned. When he did mildly broach the idea of sending Prince Henry to Scotland for safety, there was a collective sharp intake of English breath and some mutterings of censure.[12] Salisbury's view of the laws certainly remained unchanged as he told Nicolò Molin that year. It was logical, cool and disciplined: 'their object [the laws] is undoubtedly to extinguish the Catholic religion in this Kingdom, because we do not think it fit, in a well-governed monarchy, to increase the number of persons who profess to depend on the will of other Princes as the Catholics do . . .' When a Catholic wrote accusingly to Salisbury in 1606 'We know no other means left us in the world, since it is manifest that you serve but as a match, to give fire unto His Majesty . . . for intending all mischiefs against the poor distressed Catholics', the earl responded that he was not an enemy of the faith itself. Nor importantly did he hold that all of them in England harboured vast reserves of treasonable thoughts. He observed 'how little assistance was given to these late savage Papists'. He would avoid persecuting Catholics as such, but held his ground on everything else.

Nicolò Molin's uncensored despatches are helpful in establishing the mood of the nation, on the brink of a collective nervous breakdown, after this great provocation.

The King is in terror; he does not appear nor does he take his meals in public as usual. He lives in the innermost rooms with only Scotchmen [sic] about him . . . Catholics fear heretics and vice versa . . . both are armed; foreigners live in terror of their houses being sacked by the mob which is convinced that some, if not all foreign princes, are at the bottom of the plot. The King and council have very prudently thought it advisable to quiet the popular feeling by issuing a proclamation in which they declare that no foreign Sovereign had any part in the conspiracy.

Whether they actually thought this is another matter and their effort to establish the evidence either way had to be undertaken with alacrity. While they did this probe it was certainly prudent to place guards about the residences of foreign diplomats to prevent outbreaks of public wrath, an effort that had the additional attraction of possibly stemming the seepage of evidence. At this time we know the French were regarded with a lively animosity. As Molin noted in the same despatch: 'The conduct of the French ambassador is much criticised . . . because he would not wait for the letters the Queen was writing for France. He insisted on crossing on Monday [4 November] evening though the weather was bad . . . his passage was both troublesome and dangerous. They argue from this that the Ambassador, if he had not a share in the plot, at least had some knowledge of it . . .'[13]

The remarked failure of Henri IV to meet Beaumont is far from conclusive, but it is intriguing. And was there then a widely held view in French government circles that the whole plot was a fable, as one report from Paris robustly claimed? It seems unlikely, especially as the report emanated from Dudley Carleton, who

Dudley Carleton's Percy connections took time to clear. Only by 1610 had the taint of powder been eliminated

was far from neutral in his news reports, unlike the estimable Molin (whose failing was gullibility).* Carleton's training had been for public life and in 1603 while employed in Paris and not altogether happy there, he received letters from friends urging him to exploit the sound relationship he had established with the Earl of Northumberland. That he did so and successfully may have caused a wrench of displeasure later, but in 1603 he was pleased to be appointed comptroller of Percy's household and a personal secretary. This meant that he was responsible for assigning the plotters the lease for the space wherein they stored their gunpowder. When he left the earl's employ in March 1605 he worked for Lord Norris in Spain and then Paris, but his previous connection was part of the reason for his recall to London. John Chamberlain, his friend, could say that Carleton had a poor opinion of Thomas Percy, but a short spell of imprisonment and examination regarding Northumberland was inevitable. Carleton was released in December 1605 but still remained under surveillance for a time. In February 1606 he was to be found out in the Chilterns as he ruefully noted 'in order to take away the scent of powder'. In fact, it took him very much longer than he would have hoped or expected, and it was not until 1610 that he was appointed to replace Sir Henry Wotton as ambassador to Venice.

* Molin was knighted at Whitehall on 23 January 1606.

NINE

Transgression on Trial

Digby and his fellow-prisoners were brought from the Tower on a river-barge to reach Westminster about half an hour before the opening of the trial in late January 1606. Since class distinctions operated in prisons Bates was brought from the Gatehouse in Westminster itself. Together they stood waiting in star chamber for the arrival of the judges and while they were there a contemporary scrutinized them. Evidently he was displeased: 'It was strange to note their carriage, even in their very countenances.' Those who let their heads fall, bowed them, were 'full of doggedness' while those looking about them were 'forcing a stern look'; if they failed to pray this was an ugly fault, but if they did pray 'it were by the dozen upon their beads'. As for those who smoked, they were altogether too nonchalant because they did not seem to mind being hanged.[1] Sir John Harington, who was another spectator, declared: 'I have seen some of the chief [conspirators] and think they bear an evil mark in their foreheads, for more terrible countenances were never looked upon.' Taken into the hall where spectators buzzed with anticipation and all strained forward to see them, they were helpfully placed on an elevated platform in front of the judges. Queen Anne and Prince Henry were in a concealed chamber or niche from which they could see but not be seen, and it was reported inevitably that James was also somewhere present. Digby in a black satin suit and 'tuff taffetie gown' stood with the others although he was arraigned under a separate indictment from them and was tried alone after them. He would plead 'guilty', while the others pleaded 'not guilty'. According to Father Gerard, Digby's plight stirred some of the courtiers present who lamented his position 'and said he was the goodliest man in the whole court'.[2]

The first lawyer to speak for the Crown was the Master of the Rolls, Sir Edward Philips (or Phelips). The matter before the court, he said, was one of treason 'but of such horror, and monstrous nature'. To murder any man was abominable and if 'to touch God's anointed' was to oppose God himself, then 'how much more than too monstrous' was it to murder King, Queen, Prince, State and Government. After discoursing briefly on the chief points of the indictment, and describing the objects of the conspiracy and the plan, Philips sat down to make way for the principal counsel for the prosecution, Sir Edward Coke, Attorney-General for the past nine years. Educated at Norwich Grammar School, Trinity College, Cambridge and the Inner Temple, Coke had risen to prominence as prosecutor at the trial of Dr Lopez (1594) accused of planning to murder Elizabeth, and the Earl of Essex (1601), when his brutal style was

Another clumsy image that mangles topography and badly focusses on Guy Fawkes and the infamous lantern. Would the puppet show of the plot licensed by Sir George Buc in 1619 have been more sophisticated?

unrelenting. Much the same was true of his prosecution of Ralegh (1603) when his vituperation had struck many as excessive. The conspirators could be sure that he would be unsparing to the point of savagery, and even a dour spirit as redoubtable as Fawkes may have felt a pinch of disquiet as Coke rose. If Coke could discomfort them, a terror in language, he would do so. Yet he began conventionally and for him even mildly. The plot had been the greatest treason ever conceived against the greatest king that ever lived. In a rare and somewhat clumsy effort to be even-handed he went on: 'It is by some given out that they are such men as admit just exception, either desperate in estate, or base or not settled in their wits [here no doubt he gave a baleful glance towards John Grant], such as are *sine religione, sine sede, sine fide, sine re, et sine spe* [without religion, without habitation, without credit, without means, and without hope].' Yet the truth was they were men of some substance 'howsoever most perniciously seduced, abused, corrupted, and jesuited, of very competent fortunes and estates'.

Having begun with the laity, the men before him, Coke launched forth on a declamation against 'those of the spirituality' who were not yet available for trial. 'I never yet knew a treason without a Romish priest; but in this there are very many Jesuits, who are known to have dealt and passed through the whole action.'

He named four, beginning not surprisingly with Garnet, as well as 'their cursory men' like John Gerard. Working up his revulsion, he went on: 'the studies and practises of this sect principally consisted in two D's, to wit, in deposing of Kings and disposing of Kingdomes.' The effect was that 'Romish Catholics' had put themselves under 'Gunpowder Law, fit for Justices of Hell'. This in turn led him back to Roger Bacon, 'one of that Romish rabble', as the supposed inventor of the explosive material. The allusion offered two hits; 'all friars, religious, and priests were bad', but still the principal offenders were 'the seducing Jesuits . . . men that use the reverence of Religion . . . to cover their impiety, blasphemy, treason, and rebellion, and all manner of wickedness'. This last reverberating phrase was laden with deeper meaning to the more widely read in the assembly. Even a loyal (?) recusant like Anthony Copley, imprisoned on the accession of James for the Bye plot, but pardoned after a year in the Gatehouse, had warned briskly of Jesuit activities, and their pro-Spanish leanings which might lead to 'the rape of your daughter, the buggery of your son or the sodomizing of your sow'.[3]

When Coke had finished the depositions made by the prisoners on examination in the Tower were read aloud. They were humble, even penitent in tone. Thomas Winter, for example, said: 'My most honourable Lords – Not out of hope to obtain pardon, for speaking of my temporal past, I may say the fault is greater than can be forgiven . . . since I see such courses are not pleasing to Almighty God, and that all or most material parts have been already confessed.'[4] When these items had been read Popham made some remarks to the jury and directed them to consider their verdict which they did after removing to another room. Digby was then arraigned by himself upon a separate indictment charging him with high treason in conspiring the death of the king, with conferring with Catesby in Northamptonshire concerning the plot, assenting to the design and taking the oath of secrecy. As soon as the indictment was read Digby began to make a speech, but was halted and told he had to plead to the charge before launching on any sort of defence. Digby at once said he was guilty and then spoke of the motives which had led him into the action. He began with a denial that it had been ambition or discontent, or even ill-will towards any member of Parliament. Instead he put forward the commanding force of his friendship and affection for Catesby, whose influence over him was so profound that he was bound to risk his inheritance and even his life at the other's bidding. The second motive was the cause of religion, and for his faith he was glad to risk estate, life, name, memory, posterity 'and all worldly and earthly felicity whatsoever'. This is the boundless conviction of the fanatic. His third motive was prompted by the broken promises to Catholics, and had as its object the prevention of tougher laws such as they had reason to fear.[5]

Then Digby made a public petition that since the crime was his and not his family's, the punishment should be limited to him. He wanted his wife to have her jointure, his son the entailed lands, and his sisters the portions which were in his hands. He thought too of his creditors and sought permission for one of his servants to attend him to make provision for their claims. Finally, after asking pardon of the king and lords he entreated to be beheaded – the manner of a gentleman – 'that his death might satisfy them for his trespass'. Coke's response to this was as heavy and gloomy as the light in the hall at the end of a January day. He repudiated each point with sarcastic contempt and when Digby intervened to say that he had confessed he deserved the vilest death and yet 'some moderation of justice', Coke retorted sardonically that he was asking for exactly what once he had buoyantly set aside. The king showed great moderation and mercy in that for so towering a crime no new torture had been devised or inflicted. A little more in like vein and then Coke gave way to one of the commissioners, the Earl of Northampton, the learned pedant and crypto-Catholic who could bore for England.

The main thrust of his inevitably long and wordy speech was made to refute the charge against James of having broken promises to Catholics.[6] Northampton denied that James ever encouraged them to expect any favour, thus contradicting reports of Father Watson's celebrated interview with James years before in Scotland. He made too a strong point of Thomas Percy having asserted that the king had promised toleration to the Catholics – in which case why did Percy think it so worthwhile to employ Fawkes and others to plot against James in Spain? When Salisbury followed his colleague he began by acknowledging his connection by marriage with Digby, before dealing with the prisoner's plea concerning broken promises to Catholics. It imputed, of course, bad faith to James and Digby may have forfeited his beheading by simply raising the point. A proper and dignified servant of his sovereign, Salisbury rejected the charge, and when he too had finished Philips asked for the judgment of the court upon the verdict of the jury against the seven and Digby. Each man was then asked if he had anything to say as to why the sentence of death should not be pronounced against him. Thomas Winter asked for mercy for his brother Robert, who simply begged for it. Ambrose Rookwood sought rather haltingly to play down his part, being 'only persuaded and drawn in by Catesby, whom he had . . . esteemed dearer than anything else in the world'. Finally, Lord Chief Justice Popham described and defended the laws made by Elizabeth against 'priests, recusants, and receivers and harbourers of priests' and then he pronounced the usual sentence for high treason upon all eight men. Digby bowed towards the commissioners and said: 'If I may but hear any of your Lordships say you forgive me, I shall go more cheerfully to the gallows.' Their response was 'God forgive you, and we do.' By the light of flaming torches the prisoners were escorted back to the barge and thence to the Tower which they entered through Traitor's Gate. They had two days to live and meditate on their fate.[7]

In his last days Digby's resolve did not unravel. He never expressed anything until the very last but a rigid belief in what he repeatedly called 'the cause', although many priests and fellow Catholics had rehearsed both privately and publicly the condemnations made in the wake of the Bye plot. 'Oh, how full of joy should I die, if I could do anything for the cause which I love more than my life.'[8] Even writing to his sons he could not warn them to smother such transcendent yet costly feelings if their faith was under threat. Given the extent to which Catesby had manipulated and concealed details, Digby's lack of reproach or resentment seems extraordinary, but then what was important to him was the resolution he had made at the start. His sin, he declared, was not against God but

The horse-drawn hurdles of the about-to-be executed. This is a much more sophisticated image indicating a European artist who makes the whole thing a trip into the countryside rather than a piece of grim urban theatre

the state – 'I do not think there were three worth saving that would have been lost.' Evidently most people then and now did not and do not share this implacability and rightly find such a baleful attitude as evil as the serious injustices that prompted such a point of view. Certainly the revenge of the government was not going to be stalled this time by calculated royal mercy as it had been with the Main plotters. This time the monarchy had been undermined and its sacred dignity besmirched; it needed a restorative effort and 'The public execution did not re-establish justice; it reactivated power.' Such an intention could of course be undermined because in Jacobean England the frailties of the executioner and his victim might lead to an unseemly tussle between solemnity and absurdity. Indeed, there is a suspicion that the expectation of macabre farce was what continued to draw crowds, although familiarity with the grisly ritual does not seem to have reduced interest.

Digby, Robert Winter, John Grant and Thomas Bates were lashed to wattled hurdles at the Tower to be dragged lying on their backs the mile to the scaffold in St Paul's churchyard.[9] Since this was 29 January 1606, it was a cold and grubby group that was jeered at contemptuously and coarsely by curious onlookers in city streets lined with guards of householders. At the place Digby found the composure to conform to tradition by making a last speech. Now he asked forgiveness of all 'and if he had known it first to have been so foul a treason he would not have concealed it to have gained a world'. He then asked the crowd to witness that he died penitent and sorrowful. Denied the attendance of a Catholic priest, Digby rejected attentions from a Protestant clergyman.[10] He fell to prayers 'often bowing his head to the ground' before standing and saluting according to their rank all those who were near. This he managed with such an air of imperturbability 'that he appeared to be entirely fearless of death'. Then he was stripped of all garments save his shirt and he went slowly up the ladder murmuring 'O Jesus, Jesus, save me and keep me.' It seems to have been the particular unkindness of the executioner that as soon as Digby was parted from the ladder the rope was cut and he fell gashing his forehead. Perhaps he was providentially stunned before the worst. If he had been left on the noose he would not have died from strangulation because a taut rope at the end of a properly gauged drop snaps a ligament in the neck. It is this fracture which allows a boney projection to enter the base of the brain and cause death. This spontaneous event was denied Digby who was still conscious when he was hauled to the block to be castrated, disembowelled and quartered. He died (to quote *Macbeth*, I. iv. 8–11):

> As one that had been studied in his death
> To throw away the dearest thing he ow'd,
> As 'twere a careless trifle

His life, as he believed, closed and opened simultaneously. The next day, which saw the distant capture of Father Garnet after so many years, Thomas Winter, Robert Keyes, Guy Fawkes (on the brink of physical collapse) and Ambrose Rookwood were delivered in a similar fashion from the Tower. But this time the executions were at a different venue – Old Palace Yard, Westminster opposite the building that had been marked for destruction. Moving there the procession passed by a house in the Strand in which Rookwood's wife Elizabeth had secured quarters. When they got very near, Rookwood, who had been praying continuously with closed eyes now opened them to see her waiting at an open window. It is said he raised himself up from the hurdle and called to her to pray for him. She replied 'I will! I will! And do you offer yourself with good heart to God and your Creator! I yield you to Him with as full an assurance that you will be accepted of Him as when He gave you to me.'[11] Their son was actually knighted by James at the end of the reign.

Given the additional distance of Old Palace Yard from the Tower, and the lugubrious progress to it, the unhappy quartet could not summon much energy for a crowd-pleasing performance. Kneeling and often bowing their heads to the ground they prayed, but kept their voices low. Not much more than the phrase 'O Jesu, Jesu, save me and keep me' repeated continuously while on the ladder was heard. Of the four it seems to have been Keyes who retained a lingering hint of truculence. With the execution of the key plotters there was now an extended pause in the arterial wallowing. During this time Garnet, Oldcorne, Nicholas Owen and Ralph Selby were brought to the Tower, arriving on 4 February, after two days in the Gatehouse.

Garnet's first examination of many (John Gerard, SJ said twenty-three (1897)) was the following day and he maintained his cautious resistance to the questions even when the possibility of subjecting him to the rack was flourished. His reply was a steady 'Minute ista pueris' – 'Threats are only for boys.' Yet he would have learnt, because no one would have protected him from the knowledge, that Owen was marked down for torture; the warrants authorizing it were issued that month, and when he died it would have been obvious to suppose that he had succumbed to state violence, not as the government claimed, of a self-inflicted knife wound. Garnet denied having sent Baynham to the Pope and also the notion that he had encouraged Catholics to pray for the success of the 'Catholic Cause'.[12] When he admitted anything – such as the grand and obvious excursion to St Winifred's Well – it was only stuff of limited interest, and realizing the interrogations had stalled, the investigators needed to glean more without risking an immediate martyrdom. They began with the classic friendly warder option whereby a correspondence with several Catholics, including Anne Vaux, was begun, and secret notes appended in lemon juice. But the letters to her were written instead in orange juice which does not fade on heating. So to cover these specials the government needed a brilliant forger and they selected Arthur Gregory who later wrote for his reward to Salisbury, since he had been robbed of his accumulated possessions by looters during the surge of the plague in March/April of 1606. All the letters proved so guarded in their contents that nothing new emerged. Still, the warder, as if warming to his prisoners and growing more willing to serve them, allowed a door between the cells of Oldcorne and Garnet to remain unlocked, and so the men could now meet and talk. It was these conversations that were noted down for the Secretary and Northampton by Lockerson and Forsett, hidden in secret recesses. But even the most conscientious eavesdropper could not hear every word and random noises in the Tower made accuracy difficult.

Five of these brotherly chats were allowed, and for a man in such a parlous situation, Garnet showed some resilience of spirit. He was irked when an occasional snigger was the response to a pointed quip about his predicament, and he even managed to find fault with some of the questions put to him, He does, however, seem to have had a rueful respect for Coke who slid from compassion to aggression in the time-honoured fashion of interrogators through the ages. Garnet had spent some eighteen years in hiding, subduing his own recurrent fears of discovery and those of the people who gave him sanctuary. He was about fifty and had been under great strain during his long period as superior, and to some extent his attitudes had been shaped from Rome by the remote but dominating personality of Father Persons; Garnet had been 'strengthened' or hampered according to the view taken of that priest's activity. On 5 and 6 March the lord commissioners questioned Oldcorne and Garnet who at first denied having talked about the best mode of conducting their defence. Without pressure it must be unlikely that even when told that their conversations had been secretly recorded Oldcorne would have admitted with sudden candour on the second day just what exchanges he had had with his superior. Did the torturers show him what they had prepared if he remained uncommunicative, judging him the most vulnerable?

Whatever the case, Oldcorne's release of information provided the leverage for a concentrated effort to draw out Garnet and he was unable to sustain his defence. Now he admitted meeting Fawkes a year before, and writing on his behalf to Father Baldwin in the Spanish Netherlands. There were the talks as well with Catesby, now admitted, and on 9 March he wrote a declaration that he had 'dealt very reservedly with your Lordships in the case of the later powder action'. Garnet then rehearsed what he had become familiar with from colleagues – broadly speaking the known story of the plot – embellished with grace notes about his own unease as the thing developed. He had written frequently to Rome to solicit support against such wild efforts but none had been forthcoming. This is not surprising because of course Persons was at hand there. The false idea that he had moderated and adjusted his aspirations has been widely touted recently. In this view Persons had set aside activism for more emollient proceedings with James, but a further review of the evidence shows how wide of the mark this is.[13] In fact, the plot was perfectly consistent with the long-held views of the stubborn zealot. Resistance and activism had survived in the writings of Persons and were paralleled in the plot. As Garnet now revealed, the intention of the plotters had threatened many not party to it. Of the ambiguous position of Monteagle, Garnet remained uncertain but he did trail some past conversations with him to suggest anti-royal feelings and clandestine disloyalty. James was not going to allow this an airing in court and so it was suppressed.

Another examination taken by Popham, Coke, Waad and possibly Forsett, strove to pin down the Jesuit on when exactly he had had knowledge of the conspiracy. Before Easter 1605? No, late in the summer from Greenway and then directly from Catesby. It was Garnet's proposal that the Pope should be sounded and he had agreed with the choice of Baynham, having no alternative candidate. The question remained as to whether this bluff envoy was specifically briefed about the plot. Nor is it totally clear what Garnet expected of the Pope – a ban on such a violent enterprise, or something more non-commital with a hint of approval? My view is that Garnet expected Persons to have worked the papacy to an acceptance of the inevitability of violence, although Clement VIII had become increasingly irritated by the constant swirl of controversy about the English Jesuit Persons. He and Catesby were twins in the focus of their fury which was fanaticism. No doubt a vibrant component in the former's mind was the deeply buried notion of revenge on the country that had forced him into exile. As it was, Garnet's lurch into the confessional mode continued for several days, with emerging details that engaged the commissioners. Even in his unenviable position Garnet may still have hoped to avoid a charge of treason, with the substitution of the lesser misprision of treason. Then on 15 March Popham drafted a lengthy list of proofs against him which was subsequently read and annotated by Salisbury, and likely used for the trial.

When Father Baldwin was eventually returned to custody in England from the Palatinate in 1610, he maintained his innocence under examination, remaining in prison until 1618 without being tortured.[14] The government could have treated Garnet in the same way, but to build a case against the Jesuits at that time required a verdict in court on Greenway and Garnet. Since the former had escaped, the focus was bound to be on the provincial superior. Popham summarized the government line when he wrote that 'Garnet was a principal part and actor in the Gunpowder Treason, and [so too] most of the Jesuits.' Several days before this comment, Salisbury had written to the Earl of Mar asserting that Garnet 'is condemned by clear justice to have been privy to the foulest treason . . .' which actually falls short somewhat of Popham's crisp view of Garnet's centrality to the plot. By this time, as it happened, a public trial was needed as a vital decongestant of public fears in the immediate aftermath of the Great Rumour.

On 22 March at about six-thirty in the morning news swept the court (and hence London) that James had been slain at Woking and it was maintained until after nine. Double guards were set at the court gates and about the city, and Waad at the Tower was particularly galvanized. He drew up the drawbridge, shut up all his prisoners, had the great ordnance loaded and took all keys into his own possession. This seemed necessary in the light of the rumour embellishment that several courtiers had also been slain. Some said the treason was the revenge of English Jesuits, others that it had been done by Scots in drag; others still that it was the action of Frenchmen and Spaniards using a poisoned dagger. There was inevitably widespread distress, 'great weeping and lamentation both in old and young, rich and poor' until assurance of the king's safety and a proclamation to calm distracted minds. The Spanish ambassador, Zuniga, gave the Master of Ceremonies, Sir Lewis Lewkenor, a gold chain to mark the good news 'and it was thought he was so bountiful either out of terror, being afraid of the people in this confusion, because it was rumoured that the King of Spain was a fomentor of others of the Plot; or, out of a desire to vindicate his Master's honour, and take the odium from him.' In the meantime the House of Commons sat in continuous session lest a sudden rising by them should add to the general alarm. Then a messenger of the House of Lords confirmed the king's safety and perfect health, and Prince Henry led a great party to greet his father at Knightsbridge. Ordinary

Londoners flocked there too, greeting James with most impassioned rejoicing that afternoon.[15]

There followed very rapidly the trial of Father Garnet at the Guildhall on 28 March 1606, in one session lasting from 8.00 am to 7.00 pm. The discovered treatise of equivocation found among the late Francis Tresham's possessions, in a copy made for him by his servant Vavasour, with a variant title in Garnet's own hand, was to be the pivot of the proceedings, although the government still did not realize that the Jesuit was its author.[16] Garnet was trapped into defending himself on equivocation, which had never shocked English Protestants familiar with the Jesuit doctrine as deeply as it did when the Provincial of England openly espoused it. For many people a Jesuit was the agent of the devil, not of God, and 'equivocation was his means to treason'. In its pristine form the word was derived from Latin and it has passed unscathed through Middle English meaning the ability to juggle words; in *Hamlet* the gravedigger employs it so. Then it was annexed by the Counter-Reformation, continental Jesuits, to focus a technical doctrine in a particular usage. So when Cardinal Bellarmine's pupils shipped clandestinely into England (Garnet, Southwell and Oldcorne), they brought with them the invisible mental camouflage of equivocation – a colonizing agent that was an instrument of pastoral care. Southwell quoted parts of Garnet's treatise when he was put on trial in 1595. When Garnet spoke to his own defence his first reference was to equivocation which was in itself a challenge to order because it denied the differences on which order rested.[17] It justified reworking or banding the truth by the use of words with equivocal meanings, accompanied by mental reservations within a specific moral framework. Jesuits had this very flexible resource to protect themselves from magistrates wishing to interrogate them on matters which they (the Jesuits) held were not within the remit of the justices. So, if asked, a disguised priest could reply to the question 'Did you attend Mass yesterday?' with the truthful response 'No, I did not attend Mass yesterday' while silently expanding the answer with the equivocation 'at St Sepulcre's'.

The intellectual surface elasticity of Garnet's argument took the full weight of Coke's rhetoric which rolled over the defence like a great engine of siege warfare:

Although not a plotter Edward Oldcorne was the Jesuit companion of Fr Henry Garnet in hiding at Hindlip House

For equivocation, it is true indeed that they do outwardly to the world condemn lying and perjury, because the contrary were too palpable, and would make them odious to all man: but it is open and broad lying and forswearing not secret and close lying and perjury, or swearing a falsehood which is most abominable, and without defence or example. And if they allow it not generally in others, yet at least in themselves, their confederates and associates in treasonable practises, they will both warrant and defend it, especially when it may serve their turn, for such purposes and ends as they look after.

Equivocation excited particular indignation when Protestants felt so grievously agitated. Zorzi Giustinian, an anti-Jesuit Catholic, was inclined to share the Protestant viewpoint and he recorded the shock of ministers over equivocation 'and especially the King, who is particularly versed in such matters'. The jury found Garnet guilty and the death sentence was pronounced. He was then removed for further interrogations during which he continued to defend equivocation, even in the week preceding his death. Originally this was set for 1 May, but London was seething with excitement so the government felt obliged to postpone it to 3 May to avoid a clash with traditional May Day celebrations. The execution took place on a scaffold at the west end of St Paul's precinct, and as Garnet mounted the ladder, the Recorder of London, sent by James to represent him, urged the priest not to equivocate with his last breath in this life. Garnet replied with a certain rueful dignity that this was not the time to equivocate; how it was lawful and in what circumstances he had shown elsewhere. He was then hanged, but at the King's command not cut down immediately, so that he was dead when hewn apart for the affronted sovereign's superior earthly power to be demonstrated.

To many Catholics – even some who regarded equivocation with disapproval – Garnet was a martyr. Zorzi Giustinian had come to speak kindly of him, and the posthumous story of the miraculous representation of his head upon a straw in blood did honour late in 1606 to his memory. Protestants on the other hand derided the idea that Garnet was a saint and cheerfully took the view that if anything he had been a dissolute scamp. On the eve of the trial, John Chamberlain, writing to Dudley Carleton, reported that the Jesuit 'comforts himself with sack to drown sorrow' and many were willing to misunderstand Garnet's relationship with Anne Vaux. Even Salisbury teased him about this with a quip: though later he did ask Garnet's forgiveness for the ill-timed and off-colour joke. But the original accusation of clerical impropriety had a lewd charm for many others, and at his execution, as John More reported to Ralph Winwood, the Jesuit 'made many protestations endeavouring to clear the suspicion of his incontinence with Mrs Vause [sic], wherein it is thought he served himself with his accustomed equivocations . . .' This is not completely accurate because at the last Garnet was less loquacious than alleged, but More's representation chimed with contemporary views. To those Protestants who could admire composure in the face of a horrendous ritualized death, Garnet was still a traitor, as Catesby and the others had been. In the torrent of published exchanges after the government pinioned Catholics with the Oath of Allegiance (see Chapter 11), it was Bishop Andrewes who most skilfully made the government's case against Garnet. Why was the fiction of Garnet's straw being so assiduously cherished and circulated? Cardinal Bellarmine (oppressor of Galileo) called Garnet 'a man of incomparable sanctity of life', who had suffered only for refusing to reveal what his conscience forbade. To answer this Andrewes averred the contrary – that Garnet was actually a man of some notoriety for his bad habits (*'Bacchus certe magis redolebat quam Apollinum'*). And as to the gunpowder plot, he *did* know from many quarters what was intended. Even if it was admitted that he knew under the seal of confession only, there were several courses open to him. Without mentioning names he could have passed on just enough information to avert so great a crime. He might have given private information to the Pope. He might have urged the person confessing to abandon the project and induce others so to do, under threat of divulging it if the penitent refused compliance. He might have warned those whose lives were in peril. He did none of these things and so was condemned by his own actions. Indeed, by concealment he sinned, and Andrewes cited various authorities who took the view that crimes intended and communicated to a priest in confession should be revealed.

Andrewes condemned utterly any form of revolt against the legitimate power of the prince.[18] He developed this unyielding position in his famous series of sermons preached on both 5 August, in commemoration of the Gowrie plot, and 5 November. The two series began in 1606 and continued for nine and ten years respectively, so that in all there were nineteen sermons in which to ram home various concerns. Today this seems excessive but no one would have reproached Andrewes then for his submissive adulation of James. What has happened since then is that Andrewes has been judged to bear a substantial (if preliminary) responsibility for the conflict that engulfed Britain within two generations. Some historians have seen in these sermons the ideological basis for the combined errors of William Laud and Charles I, since Andrewes held the unshakeable conviction that all power derived from God and any prince of any sort had 'the mandate of heaven'. Proverbs 8:15 'By me Kings reign'. God alone makes or unmakes a prince, and no one on his own authority can substitute for God. So Andrewes condemned the theories that had arisen to revise the fundamental stance he took: the papal pretension to the right of deposition; the notion of the 'social contract', and any form of rebellion at all.[19] His position required passive obedience to tyranny and the renunciation of any resistance; those who rejected this stance were condemned for the thought and subsequent action. In his sermons Andrewes would sometimes invite his listeners to give thanks to God for the physical destruction of the Gowrie and the gunpowder plotters, as well as pray for the ultimate destruction of the king's enemies. He viewed both plots in the same light and his sermons did not differentiate between them. As far as the gunpowder plot was concerned he gave voice to the view of a large section of public opinion, emphasizing its unprecedented intention to kill in an instant such a throng of people. The suddenness of it appeared particularly terrible since unprepared souls were at risk. Such thoughts gave his oratory its keenness – with a personal edge to it. On Sunday 3 November 1605 he had been consecrated Bishop of Chichester and appointed Lord High Almoner. On 5 November he resigned his Mastership of Pembroke Hall, Cambridge, and thus ended a thirty-five year connection begun when he entered the college as a student. Now fifty, this huge change in his life might have marked its end, for as a bishop he would have been in the House of Lords.[20]

TEN

The Second Wave

When Thomas Wilson, nephew of Queen Elizabeth's principal secretary of that same name, prepared a list of her possible successors at home and abroad, he favoured James VI over Lady Arabella Stuart.[1] Even so, he did not exclude Henry Percy, ninth Earl of Northumberland whose claim was based on his descent from a grand-daughter of the eldest brother of Henry III. A plot that killed the Stuarts *en masse*, as well as many of the aristocracy, would likely have left him as the highest ranking living Englishman in the country, and with a large Catholic following. One drawback by the late sixteenth century was that the Percy family had something of a reputation for scepticism, and the earl's particular interest in science, his strong patronage of Thomas Hariot and others, in combination made him an object of some suspicion. He was not quite right somehow, and his easy sarcasm and pointed wit left him somewhat isolated at court. There was also the undeniable fact that he regarded the Scots who clustered tightly about James with a contempt which as a northern earl he made no effort to hide: 'a disdainful and contemptuous attitude which could not fail to make him many enemies at court.' By 1605 Northumberland had withdrawn more and more into the company of congenial friends, including Thomas Percy. This made him a target the moment the news of the plot broke. John Chamberlain, writing to Dudley Carleton, once in the earl's employ, quickly remarked on this. His fears were justified because on 27 November James signed the warrant to commit the earl to the Tower to await trial. His brothers, Sir Allan and Sir Josceline were also arrested, along with hitherto privileged Catholic lords like Mordaunt, Stourton and Montagu. The second of these was a kinsman of Salisbury, while Montagu was the son-in-law of the Lord Treasurer, the Earl of Dorset. Of the trio it was Montagu who was least marked by suspicion, although on the Tuesday before All Saints' Day (29 October) he had met Catesby at the Savoy. Their mild and brief exchanges were noted by Montagu in a letter of explanation to his powerful father-in-law: 'The Parliament,' said Catesby, 'I think bringeth your lordship up now?' Montagu: 'No surely; but it will on Monday next, unless my Lord Treasurer do obtain me his Majesty's licence to be absent which I am in some hope of.' Then Catesby said something to the effect that Montagu could hardly be entranced by such business, and his lordship agreed. The rest of the conversation seems innocuous enough being 'of my walks (as I remember)' and 'of maintaining them'. Is there possibly something encoded in this or was Catesby really interested in the maintenance of Montagu's formal gardens? Perhaps he was planning something at Ashby St Legers? At any rate, Montagu was released from custody later in the year after some lobbying. For Mordaunt and Stourton there were problems with a statement made by Fawkes that Catesby had known that neither man would be in Parliament on the day. Suspicions about them lingered and Drayton House was described as 'a receptacle of most dangerous persons'. After a star chamber hearing they were fined and imprisoned. The nineteen privy councillors and judges set Mordaunt's fine at 10,000 marks (£6,666) and Stourton's at 6,000 (£4,000). These massive demands were never cleared and both men were removed from the Tower to the Fleet prison in August 1606. Stourton was released in 1608, while Mordaunt, who had had the most frequent contacts with the plotters, died in the following year.[2]

In the meantime the government had the not inconsiderable problem of deciding whether to deal with Northumberland in the same manner, or to embark upon a trial for treason. The slow build-up of anecdotal evidence permitted the preparation of a case for either sort of prosecution and certainly Salisbury was wary of jumping to conclusions. He wrote to Sir Thomas Edmondes in early December that while Thomas Percy might have given his kinsman some generalized warning of what was being prepared, there was 'no direct proof whether the Earl would have been present at Parliament or not . . .'. Others were less cautious and Sir William Browne, lieutenant-governor of Flushing, whose daughter had married a Percy, was stung into writing from there on 9 November: 'Seeing the earl of Northumberland hath so villainously and devilishly forgot himself, I am sorry that ever I honoured him, and more sorry that I have a child that carries his name.' So at home and abroad the earl's involvement was often assumed and he was correct to become apprehensive for he was indeed trapped. Salisbury noted his misfortune; Catesby and Thomas Percy were dead together, so the earl's 'innocency or his guiltiness must both depend upon the circumstances of other persons and times'. As the case against him grew the earl was hot in his own defence and so too was his wife. Although Salisbury seems to have maintained a private view until the beginning of March 1606 that Northumberland was innocent, Dorothy Percy, his countess, one of the famous sisters of Essex, boldly put it to James that only he could deflect 'the ill-will of a certain great personage'.

The king went no further than a retreat from the idea of a state trial for treason, which was hardly likely to please her ladyship, even if her husband thus escaped her brother's fate. When Montagu, Mordaunt and Stourton had been dealt with, the government could not leave the earl in a judicial limbo, and hence on 26 June he was tried in star chamber for three complaints that seem to have been admitted. There was a charge of seeking to lead English Catholics and secure toleration for them. Another of having written letters during his detention that were disrespectful of the king's service. And perhaps the most serious charge of all was that Thomas Percy had been permitted to join the select company of the king's gentlemen pensioners without taking the oath of supremacy – neither the earl nor his deputy had tendered the oath. As Coke described matters he no doubt induced a shiver – Thomas Percy had been daily in the king's presence with a halberd in his hand 'a thing most dangerous for such a person'. This was Coke's last effort as attorney-general and the public humiliation of a great man made fine sport for the spectators. There was intense public interest again, although the size of the star chamber did not allow all to enter who sought admission.

Coke was saturated in the details of the government case and so thoroughly rehearsed in these trials that there can have been no doubt that Northumberland would be found guilty. He had for some time been a figure at court whose presence created a certain unease by his inclination to sarcasm and his open sneers at the Scots who had come south with James. The earl had a haughty unyieldingness that caused offence and in the special circumstances of a trial all the advantage lay with the monarch. There was even the problem for Northumberland of his deafness and stutter, which under pressure may have become exaggerated and so veiled what he needed to say clearly. The judges reached a consensus on the appropriate punishment after Dorothy Percy's uncle, Lord Knollys, had suggested the sum of £20,000 as a fine. This was upped to £30,000 – the largest ever demanded of an Englishman to that date – and the earl lost his place on the privy council, his office as captain of the gentlemen pensioners and was imprisoned at the king's pleasure.[3] Zorzi Giustinian took the view of many that the earl fully deserved the judgment. 'The proofs of his complicity in the plot are overwhelming, and he was saved', wrote the ambassador to the Doge on 12 July, 'only by the grace of the king.'[4] It was all a great shock to the earl who had expected to be acquitted 'but when he saw the case going against him he became so alarmed that he returned unsatisfactory answers, and such as were not expected from a man of his prudence and intelligence.' It was also a terrible and humiliating blow to Lady Percy, whose spirited lobbying gained her a fearsome reputation. Even the notably patient Salisbury could flinch with irritation at being constantly challenged by her 'sour dealing'.

The earl was evidently taken aback at the trial by the Crown's delineation of Thomas Percy's actions, which he now heard fully outlined for the first time. Many other people in the Catholic community also found the whole matter of the plot, its public exposure and subsequent trials profoundly unsettling. The notoriety of it was such that every aspect was treated with the utmost seriousness, testing administrative networks and procedures almost to their limits. What was so disturbing for the government was that there was not just one locus for the threat as there had been with the Essex revolt, nor just one quite clear cluster of dissidents. They were continually finding second and third tiers of accomplices and friendly aides who feared for their own safety, and yet risked all to shelter fugitives. When Robert Winter and Stephen Littleton were at last taken as they prepared to flee abroad, they emerged from the hitherto safe house of Littleton's cousin in Hagley (Worcestershire) where they had mingled freely with his large household of at least ten tenants. So not only were the two wanted men imprisoned but Humphrey Littleton and three other Hagley citizens were imprisoned as well. Only the former was spared while he prepared a written deposition detailing a Jesuit underground network and accusing five more people. There were local trials all over the West Midlands: Henry Morgan and Stephen Littleton were executed at Stafford; John Winter died at Red Hill near Worcester, with Humphrey Littleton (Perkes and his man Barford were executed at the same time).

A chastened recusant Ben Jonson sought to aid the government (and himself) in the aftermath of the plot

Revulsion and angry disillusionment, reinforced by the details published with government authority after the trials, led not a few to spurn the church that had recently won them. Having adopted Catholicism 'by trust of a priest' the playwright Ben Jonson now sought pardon for his recusancy from the Bishop of London on 20 April 1606. In the time of distress some felt the tempest threatening to blow them off their feet and into prison, and it is possible to consider in some detail one example that must stand for many. Sir Henry James (knighted in 1603 since recusancy had never prevented it), completed the civic and church formalities for submission and conformity with a remarkable alacrity. It took ten days – 24 May to 6 June – to carry out all the complicated requirements. To obtain the official ecclesiastical recognition of his conformity, his case was heard in the consistory court of the Bishop of London on 31 May, probably at Old St Paul's. His offence was that over the previous three months he had refused to attend the services in St Sepulcre, his parish church, or any substitute. Sir Henry made his declaration to the court that he had been a recusant, but had changed his mind and now sought to be absolved from his excommunication. Two witnesses for him signed a certificate attesting to his conformity a week before when on Saturday and Sunday he had gone to Westminster Abbey and St Paul's for a high-profile reconciliation. To the presiding official he presented a letter of support from the curate of St Sepulcre's who attested 'that he found him a gentleman very willing to join with the Church of England in holy service to God and to be hereafter obediently comfortable to the laws of God and his prince.' James promised his future obedience under oath and having done so was promptly absolved and restored to the communion of the English church. Still, evidence of his attendance at a service in St Sepulcre's was required and he went the following day having alerted the incumbent of his intention so that he could obtain from him a signed certificate of attendance.

This item was handed to the church court by midday, but the business was not yet completed. There followed an interview with the bishop who had to give Sir Henry the signed and sealed certificate of conformity required for discharge at the exchequer. This was handed over on Sunday afternoon, probably at the bishop's town house in St Paul's churchyard. Sir Henry was now ready to face the exchequer and he took Monday to gather himself before his presentation on Tuesday 3 June to the revenue court at Westminster Hall. There he asked for a discharge of his modest outstanding debt of £100 and the ending of all penalties for recusancy which he had now abjured. The certificate of the bishop was read out and Sir Henry ended his petition with the claim that by virtue of Statute 28 Elizabeth, c. 1, his proven conformity entitled him to a full discharge. His plea was then supported by Coke himself, who must have savoured such an event as the ripe consequence of his own work against the confessional dissidents. The barons of the exchequer accepted these submissions and gave Sir Henry his discharge after a hectic few days. The authorities were satisfied, but in an ironic reversal Sir Henry found his family very much more unwilling to accept such a change. His wife, Lady Dorcas, offered most spirited opposition despite his hectoring and bluster, a situation that only grew worse when their children sided with her. As a 'battered' wife she quit the family home in Kent and looked for refuge with her Protestant elder sister, Lady Alice Carew, who could not approve of Catholicism, but responding to unhappiness offered protection and money. Lady Dorcas fretted about the children, especially her youngest daughters, Martha, Aurea and Catherine, whom their father placed as boarders with a London schoolmistress before they shifted again to be united with their mother. Happily the family rift did mend by November 1607, and then began the gradual decay of Sir Henry's new found Protestantism. By 1611, when he and Lady Dorcas were living in the family town house in Turnmill Street they were both charged and convicted of recusancy. A case where the family that prayed together, stayed together.[5]

The maladroitness of the gunpowder plotters, their discovery and the trials naturally disposed Parliament to an even more unyielding implementation of anti-Catholic policy. Early in 1606 new laws regarding priests and their followers were considered and James himself told the departing Nicolò Molin: 'I shall, most certainly, be obliged to stain my hands with their blood, though sorely against my will.' Yet Salisbury noted that his own colleagues in the House of Lords, as well as the king, wanted a more merciful policy than the House of Commons. When Parliament rose for the summer in June 1606, the new penal code had become law. Two Acts against recusants sharpened the old legislation and added new provisions, so the nigh-on manic desire of Sir Henry James to ditch his old allegiance becomes understandable. The justification of the government for this tightening on recusancy coincided with the moment when Venice was excommunicated by the papacy, a move that reinforced the view in London that civil obedience and loyalty to Rome were incompatible. One of the leading figures in Venetian political and religious life was Father Paolo Sarpi, soon to be Theological Counsellor to the Serene Republic, a man of influence, with Protestant contacts all over Europe. One of the Englishmen with whom he had had many exchanges was Sir Edwin Sandys whom he helped with the writing of *Europae Speculum*, a 'temperate but penetrating analysis of the influence of the Church of Rome in Europe'. It was Sandys and Sir Charles Perkins who moved a Cecilian amendment in Parliament to prevent the archdukes from recruiting to their armies, although the Somerset House treaty (1604) allowed them to do this. Salisbury could stifle recruitment in England but as he knew very well from his sources Ireland was a different matter. The unruliness of the Irish was a source of real concern to London, as was their continued recruitment by the archdukes. Sir Arthur Chichester, viceroy of Ireland, noted the increasing numbers of 'loose men of this nation' flocking to the Spanish Netherlands. In June 1606 the Irish regiment under Colonel Henry O'Neill (son of the Earl of Tyrone) was already reported to be between 1,000 and 1,200, and by the time of the second anniversary of the gunpowder plot, Edmondes put the figure at between 1,600 and 1,700 men. He was also irked by the strength of clerical influence within both the Irish and English infantries of the archdukes, and it seems to have been enough to trigger the block on recruiting. The ambassador noted with dismay that promotion and good commands within these regiments largely depended on being obsequious to Father Baldwin, Hugh Owen and others of their clique, that is to say Jesuits and priests, the very sort of men the two Acts of Parliament

against recusancy held responsible for the instigation and encouragement of the
gunpowder plot.

An Act for the better discovery and repressing of Popish Recusants (3 Jac. I, cc.
4 and 5, Statutes of the Realm IV, 1071–82), reiterated the old regime of
Elizabethan fines and restrictions and introduced a sacramental test and a new
oath known as the Oath of Allegiance.[6] According to James it was 'ordained for
making difference between the civilly obedient Papists and the perverse disciples
of the Powder Treason'. In the matter of fines a convicted recusant who had
conformed for a year had to take communion annually or be liable (£60 for a
refusal). In a sense this was a device to see if someone like Sir Henry James was
actually a conforming crypto-papist, but there was another tougher provision, a
fine of £10 per month was to be exacted from all persons keeping servants who
absented themselves from church. The statute forbidding recusants to go more
than five miles from their homes was confirmed and they were now prohibited
from practising at the Bar, acting as attorneys or physicians, 'from executing
trusts committed to them as executors of a will or acting as guardians of minors'
(often a lucrative enterprise for the unscrupulous). Of central interest to James
was the oath of allegiance, which required clusters of citizens like recusants, non-
communicants and transients to acknowledge him as their lawful sovereign, and to
deny that the Pope had any power to depose him, authorize invasions by foreign
princes of his dominions, or free his subjects from their allegiance. The theory of
the Divine Right of Kings so passionately upheld by James was a very important
item in the struggle for national rights against the papacy, and these new statutes
were props for this over-arching notion. The struggle for freedom from papal
interference was still going on across Europe, and the Roman controversialists
who had given up their hopes of converting James still disputed his claim to the
throne. Father Persons, as it has been shown, was just such a papalist.

The oath was to be taken without equivocation or mental reservation, and no
one, not even the Pope, had any power to grant absolution from it. If a recusant
refused to take the oath when it was tendered to him by a bishop or two justices of
the peace, he/she was to be gaoled and held there without bail until the next
court session. Refusal to take the oath then incurred the penalty of praemunire:
deprivation of all civil rights; loss of all property, and perpetual imprisonment.*
That those who were punished for refusing to submit to these laws could not in
James's opinion be considered as suffering 'for conscience in matter of religion'
was made clear a decade later in his speech to the judges in star chamber. There
was the usual gratuitous protest that he was loath to hang a priest only for
religion's sake and saying mass; 'but if he refuse the oath of allegiance which (let
the Pope and all the devils in Hell say what they will) . . . is merely civil, those
that so refuse the oath and are polypragmatic recusants I leave them to the law; it
is no persecution but good justice.' As James had said, the point of the legislation

---

* A papal nuncio to Spain in the 1580s had called praemunire 'bestial'. It was among laws in
England 'most prejudicial to the apostolic authority' and he longed to see it abolished, 'when by
God's grace we get the upper hand.'

was to make a distinction between Catholics with quiet dispositions who were good subjects, and those who thought (and might even act) along the lines of the plotters. The oath formula, approved by Parliament and with royal sanction was positioned within a framework of over seventy articles. It was designed to achieve multiple objectives and evidently one aim was the application of a veneer of legality to the plundering of private Catholic wealth. How much still there was of that has already been outlined in various individual cases.

To go after such wealth was not simply greedy opportunism – although it was also that. The parlous state of royal finances was always a profound concern to James's ministers. Whatever his protestations they were too often at variance with his actions for a buoyant reserve. James was both unwilling and unable to check his liberality – kingship required an open purse, and in the first four years of his reign he distributed £68,000 in gifts, £30,000 in pensions, and debts to the Crown of £174,000 had been pardoned. Between 1603 and 1612 James also managed to spend £185,000 on jewels.[7] Not surprising then that all monetary sources had to be squeezed and that Catholics figured prominently on the list. Among those who suffered were Anne Vaux and her nephew, Lord Vaux. She was 'called to the sessions at Newgate and there for refusing that oath, was condemned in a praemunire, to lose all her goods and lands during her life, and to perpetual imprisonment.' In March 1612, John Chamberlain wrote to Carleton that Lord Vaux was lately committed to the Fleet by the privy council for following her example. What happened was that in May he was condemned and imprisoned in King's Bench and only the entreaties of influential friends brought a diminution of his punishment, so that by October he had been pardoned of the praemunire and delivered to the custody of the Dean of Westminster 'to see what good may be done with him'. Efforts to influence Lord Vaux did not in fact succeed until February 1626. Long before that it was Salisbury who deliberately yoked the need of the state for money to the danger of the Church from the recusants. He took an active part in pushing through the oath legislation and was probably not above mild massaging of threats to his own person for political ends. The result was a fiscal triumph because in a unique sign of loyalty in time of peace Parliament granted James three subsidies and six fifteenths.

ELEVEN

'Sharp Additions'

The Oath of Allegiance was very cannily drafted and at least one historian who probed its recesses thought it 'a masterpiece of political wizardry'.[1] The ingenuity of its phrasing suggests collaboration between the king, the earls of Salisbury and Northampton and Archbishop Bancroft. The Secretary of State had by that time achieved a rare regard (popularity would be too strong a word) among the public that was manifested in the great concourse of people who attended him as he made his way to be installed as a Knight of the Garter. Sir Henry Neville attributed this swell to Salisbury's 'constant dealings in matters of religion . . .' and since admission to the oldest and most prestigious chivalric order was within the monarch's gift, it is certain that James was now well pleased with his chief minister. On advice (Perkins may have helped with the wording) Salisbury and those about him had devised an oath wherein 'the supremacy of the king would be practically acknowledged and the connection of the English Catholics with the Papacy dissolved'. It will be remembered that the popes in the Middle Ages had been granted by common consent a certain authority over civil rulers and that under special conditions this included the right of deposition.[2] With only a few exceptions theologians of the early seventeenth century recognized the legitimacy of these rights. Even so, there was no unanimity on their origin and limits or the advisability of using them. The Appellants' 'Protestation of Allegiance' (1603) had been condemned by the theological faculty of Louvain precisely because it expressed a denial of the indirect powers of the Pope in temporal matters. No Catholic could deny a doctrine so widely taught; to swear the oath would be to go way beyond this.

'I do from my heart abhor, detest and abjure, as impious and heretical, this damnable doctrine and position, that princes which be excommunicated or deprived by the pope may be deposed or murdered by their subjects or any other whatsoever.'

This is a typical example of the perplexing ambiguities contained in the formula, since a Catholic was bound by his faith to deny that a prince could be murdered. Refusal to swear then would mark a person as potentially a denizen of evil, while the clause is threaded with other decidedly objectionable declarations. To pronounce the sentence cited, without qualification, would be tantamount to declaring that for centuries the Church had taken a benign view of heretical doctrine. Moreover, since the oath was sanctioned by the monarch and administered in his name, the juror seems to be locked into acknowledging a

Protestant monarch's right to set the bounds of orthodoxy. James could and did scoff at this reading, but Catholics had no reason to be optimistic that such would not be the official response once they had submitted. The immediate reaction of the laity to the proclamation of the oath ranged from desperation to uneasy bewilderment. We have seen how Sir Henry James flung himself into the effort to quit an already persecuted minority, but according to the view of the French ambassador '[Catholics] are still incredibly numerous, and are resolved for the most part to suffer anything rather than give up their religion.'³ Yet the harshness of the new laws was a profound shock to most of them and caused widespread fear and anxiety. Boderie again: 'Many Catholics are preparing to go into exile, and among them some so old that I think they are seeking foreign shores merely to find there a peaceful grave.' He admired those who stalwartly remained, feeling a surge of pride that they showed so much fervour and zeal. He recorded too some surprise at unexpected signs of religious vitality, with clandestine Catholics declaring themselves openly every day. It was a resolute response that fell away somewhat during the summer months, for a different assessment was recorded in August by the Venetian ambassador who described the courageous efforts of the majority of the clergy to stiffen the shrinking Catholic resistance. The retreat from confrontation was apparent to Father Jones writing to Robert Persons in October: 'It is scarce credible what difficulty we have to keep up and underprop poor afflicted souls from ruin, and falling into errors and disorders, and all by reason of these late cruel laws.'⁴

This shift of opinion and resolution among lay Catholics requires some explanation. The agent for such a transmutation was Archpriest George Blackwell, one of whose assistants, Father John Mush, arrived in London shortly after the prorogation of Parliament. Mush found his co-religionists in turmoil over the oath legislation with divisions in their opinions as to whether Catholics could in good conscience pronounce the formula. In a series of conferences Blackwell strongly resisted the opinion of some he canvassed that there had to be a way of satisfying the government without compromising their own tenets of faith, and he was supported by Mush, the Benedictine Thomas Preston and the Jesuit superior, Richard Holtby. By Mush's account he tried to persuade Blackwell at this time to send a delegation to Rome for papal scrutiny of this and other matters causing woe, or to hold a conference of representatives of the secular clergy, Jesuits and Benedictines to fashion a binding response for all. Blackwell refused these courses, saying it was too dangerous for him personally. This did not sit well with the others who naturally protested that they too were in jeopardy. With the whole future of the Catholic Church in England under threat, they were willing to risk arrest and exile for the sake of ensuring a united sacerdotal cluster against a hostile government.⁵

What a shock then for all, perhaps even for the agent of it, when Blackwell suddenly shunned his former ardently held position, and presented the reverse view. Having inveighed against the oath he now equally vigorously defended taking it. Much persuasion was required to get him round now to the idea of a conference – which actually meant a roundtable discussion with three of his assistants, Bishop, Broughton and Mush – together with Preston and Holtby. To them Blackwell explained his dramatic volte-face: the Church would be harmed rather than helped as a result of a pontifical declaration of deposition against the king, so the Pope had not the power to depose him. With this in mind they could swear that the Holy See was without authority and jurisdiction. Not so, said Mush, Holtby and Preston, as Bishop and Broughton sided with the archpriest, now very reluctant to hear any arguments that contradicted his view. Evidently the exchanges went on for some time and the encounter finally petered out with the opposing parties still divided over how to proceed. It was a muddled business that had dangerous elements of future schism in it unless promptly resolved by an authoritative pronouncement, so Mush and his colleagues put the business before Rome.

There was in the interim no possibility of a news blackout in London where word spread rapidly that the archpriest had now sanctioned the taking of the oath. It was a source of wonder to many and to ease the flap the three priests who had opposed Blackwell felt obliged for the sake of peace and unity to explain the superior's attitude to anyone seeking advice and comfort. They were, of course, permitted to follow him if they chose, but within a few days Blackwell was taken aback by reports that many of the secular clergy, all of the Jesuits and Benedictines, as well as a hefty number of the laity found his interpretation of the oath quite unfathomable. It was an impressive response and so Blackwell edged back to a more neutral position – that Catholics would do better to refrain from taking the oath until the Pope's decision was known to London. But in the matter of timing of his earlier pronouncement something unlooked for had happened, and now it was too late to counteract as effectively as he would have wanted the second response to his original statement. Already the Catholics who had journeyed to London for the Trinity session of the law courts were on their way home spreading the first report through the country. In a surge of relief, many Catholics, particularly those geographically isolated, took the oath without faltering when it was first administered to them. Those in doubt about their duty were naturally inclined to accept the report of the archpriest's decision as final and conduct themselves accordingly. Even those who had determined not to take the oath would be strongly counter-inclined if pushed to change their mind, by the thought of protecting themselves against the heavy penalties. In addition all of them had to be very cautious in using the few means of communication that were open to them to circulate the reversed decision, which many were slow to believe. Indeed, Blackwell seems to have skipped official notification of his people of the new plan, which is surely very suggestive of the way he was thinking. When Holtby wrote to Persons in Rome on 30 October he remarked: 'The customer [code for Blackwell] doth now insinuate unto his friends that his opinion is contradicted, and excuseth his error: yet doth he not apprehend it so sensitively that he thinketh himself bound to reveal it, though it hath caused an exceeding scandal, and will do still until the breve come: until which time he will rest quiet.'

The keenly awaited papal letter of Paul V must have arrived shortly after, since it was dated 22 September 1606. In it, the Pope declared that Catholics could not lawfully take the oath because it contained 'many things contrary to faith and salvation'. Holtby, who had sent a copy of the oath formula to Rome immediately after its publication, seems to have been the first to have received an authentic copy of the papal document. He passed it to Blackwell who showed it to a few of his friends, but declined to act despite the restrained clamour of others. His excuse was that at seventy he was unwilling to thrust his head knowingly into a noose. He made this statement to Archbishop Bancroft and a panel of bishops at a Lambeth Palace examination in the summer of 1607. The many intelligencers and spies who sought sensitive information and items for the government were busy, and someone came upon a copy of the papal brief as the Catholic population entered a period of severe anxiety. They were waiting for a dramatic and crushing enforcement of the new laws. Yet for weeks on end nothing happened and the imagined oppression was held off. The likeliest explanation for this mild hiatus appears to be that Bancroft had won over James, inducing him to hold the laws in suspension until he could prevail upon a sufficiently large number of the secular clergy, with whom he had clandestine contacts, to approve the oath, hoping after to mop up the laity. The progress of this faltered early in 1607 when Bancroft was alerted to evidence that the missionaries had succeeded in persuading many to stand firm in their deep coupling to Rome. The archbishop tried then to counter this by inducing an unhappy and agitated archpriest to write to his clergy: 'I persuade myself that you, my assistants and dear brethren, will take the oath as I have done, and that you will instruct the lay Catholics that they may do so when it is offered to them.' So when Zorzi Giustinian wrote a despatch in August of that year it is no surprise to read: 'The Catholics here are in a flutter since the archpriest has taken the oath of supremacy [i.e. allegiance] and has exhorted others to do the same, a step that is directly contrary to the brief which was addressed to the English Catholics. Everyone is in doubt about the matter. . . .'

But then no one was in doubt by 1610. On 2 June a royal proclamation was issued with a lengthy but usefully detailed title: A proclamation for the due execution of all former laws against recusants, giving them a day to repair to their dwellings, and not afterward to come to the court, or within ten miles of London without special licence; and disarming them as the law requireth; and withal, that all Priests and Jesuits shall depart the land by a day, no more to return into the realm; and for administering the oath of allegiance according to the law. A statute reinforced the decree (7 Jac 1, c. 6, Statutes of the Realm) and required the oath be taken 'by all and every person and persons'. This time no exemptions were made in favour of the nobility as had been done in 1606. The penalty of praemunire was called up for them as for all others who refused to submit within six months of the passage of the bill. No time was now wasted and the privy council had themselves immediately to take the oath in James's presence as a way of setting things in motion. After them everyone within the palace was sought out, and all government officials in high as well as low positions, professional men and students were required to follow suit. Even servants of those in the House of Lords who took the oath were obliged to follow their employers, and anyone who refused was sacked.

Making an estimate of the number of Catholics in Parliament during the post-plot reign of James, has its pitfalls. Scrutiny of the parliamentary Journals suggests that very few Catholics sought a seat in the Commons. Apart from the fact that their faith made their chances of success rather meagre, there was another deterrent – the House rule that all MPs should receive communion in an Anglican church. But there was no requirement in law for this and quite often the matter was disregarded. Moreover, although the oath was administered at the beginning of every session, a nimble Catholic could avoid this and after occupy his seat. So in 1610 it was only after twenty members had simply repeated the formula which was read by the clerk that someone questioned the legality of such procedure. Discussion followed and although some remained dubious it was generally thought to have been lawfully administered. The first day of the session was always confused and buzzing, and as John Pym noted much later in his diary 'Divers did escape without taking the Oath at all.' It is similarly impossible to be exact about numbers of Catholic peers in the House of Lords, although early in the nineteenth century the figure of twenty was regarded as reasonable. Of these, eight subscribed sometime during the session of 1610, but an almost equal number stalled and took years to comply, while still others refused. Lord Lumley, who was listed as present in 1610, had died the previous year, so that leaves four, including the earls of Shrewsbury and Worcester, declining to take the oath in public. By 1624 the personalities had changed but the numbers remained the same, with four being expelled from the Lords for persistently refusing the oath. Before the end of the session three (Lords Morley, Montagu and the Earl of Arundel) were induced to submit, but Francis Manners, Earl of Rutland, held out for over two years. For years he had haunted the court and become something of a curiosity, even a privy councillor in 1617 when James was trying to impress the Spanish ambassador. But Rutland's religion undoubtedly held back his public career as he profited little from his ambitions. Perhaps because of this he was ready to pay a very heavy price for the marriage of his daughter Katherine to James's favourite, the Marquis of Buckingham, who got £10,000 in cash and the reversion of lands that had a yearly rental in thousands and an income of even more. Clearly some Catholic aristocrats could still muster huge sums even after years of legislation devised to be punitive.[6]

Those privileged by birth and great wealth could in some measure remove themselves from heavy scrutiny. As for the great majority of Catholics, Father George Birkhead, appointed in 1608 to replace the imprisoned Blackwell and writing in July 1610 to Rome, noted 'The new oath is so pressed by the king that it causeth many to stagger.' The Venetian ambassador thought the same: 'They are proceeding against the Catholics with unusual vigour' he wrote in December that year. Such anecdotal evidence was corroborated by many missionaries. At the March sessions of gaol delivery in 1612, twenty-two Catholics were imprisoned in Newgate, having been tried and condemned to praemunire for refusing the oath. Eleven other prisoners listed as 'recusant papists' seem to have been committed for the same offence, though not yet convicted. In the following year they were all still there and their number had increased by seven. Out of London – in, for example, Nottinghamshire – the majority of Catholics who were called to take the oath preferred instead to suffer the penalties rather than violate their consciences. In the south-west of England in contemporary calendars for Devonshire (which can be regarded as representative), there were many instances of people being imprisoned for praemunire stemming from refusal to take the oath. It was tendered without partiality to anyone who had given cause for suspicion, and the general picture formed from an examination of a variety of records has revealed that the oath was imposed with much greater rigour in the south than the north. For a brief period after the enactment of the legislation officials were mostly prompt in directing it as necessary. So in September 1607 the Bishop of Durham informed James that he had summoned more than twenty noted recusants of whom six took the oath at once, a few others promised to take it, and the rest were undecided. The following year in Yorkshire it was reported that 'Thirty persons have been stripped of their goods and condemned to imprisonment for life for refusing this oath.' Subsequently, however, the justices slackened so much in their duty that they were frequently called to task by the judges of assize. One of the most intriguing items of evidence in this period stems from a performance in Yorkshire in 1609 by a travelling company of provincial actors. Their play set out the life of St Christopher and the players and audience alike were Catholics. All responded robustly to the ridicule heaped on the state Church, and the play spread disaffection among its hearers.[7]

In one respect the legislation was even-handed, for women were treated no more lightly than men. In 1612, Thomas Chamberlain, who later became a judge, reported to the Lord Chancellor Ellesmere on his efforts to enforce it.

'I, with the Justices of the division beyond Oxon, went to Sir Francis Stonor's house, [the Chamberlains and Stonors were kinsmen] when his lady, the Lady Lentall his daughter, Mrs Crouch his sister, and the Lady Lentall's woman, refused to take the oath of allegiance, and thereupon we committed them all to prison.' They went on to Henry Stonor's residence and his wife had quit the home in advance of their arrival 'because she would not take the oath'. From there they passed on to Mr Symonds, 'a man of great estate' who reported the same about his wife. Chamberlain and Sir George Tipping then continued their sweep to Mr Belson's, where the husband and wife were both recusants. This time Belson had removed himself, and his wife, his mother, the wife of a Mr Lovatt and a Mrs Belson tactfully classed as 'an ancient maid', all refused to take the oath and were briskly sent to prison.[8] There were many such instances of women being subjected to real suffering as a result of oath legislation. Catholic women married to non-Catholic men saw their families plunged into distress because they held firm to their beliefs. One woman (the story was told by John Chamberlain in a letter to Dudley Carleton) was so tormented by her husband's unremitting insistence that she submit and 'have her children otherwise educated', that she killed them and was herself then condemned and executed. Even the courtroom gave such women no protection from ill-considered vilification, and on one recorded occasion when drunk, the Master of the Rolls, Sir Edward Philips, berated a woman by 'calling her all the lewd names of whore, drab, queen, which he could devise'. Having asked if he could hang her, he settled eventually for praemunire 'and committed her to perpetual imprisonment.' The rigours of prison existence often hastened the death of those detained, and penalties were only rarely lightened in favour of the aged and infirm; Father Mush's sister and brother, approaching seventy years, were likewise condemned 'and suffered utter shipwreck of lands and goods . . .'.

In the period from 1607 to 1616 it is certain that thirteen Catholics lost their lives as a result of the oath. So it may be said that Catesby and his disciples to a very great extent accounted for one each. It seems, moreover, probable that there were cases that for various reasons went unrecorded, so the culpability of the plotters was even greater. In some instances refusal to take the oath was the principal or sole charge; in every case the condemned person was promised a remission of the death penalty if he (or she) would pronounce the prescribed formula. However, there is also abundant evidence that submission to it did not always, or even usually, bring relief from other penalties, and the government was not satisfied that it should merely be done once. The requirement that the oath be taken repeatedly often entailed great hardship and extended suffering. In 1615 it was reported of Coke (then Lord Chief Justice) that he was always rendering the oath. 'He is said to have summoned to this time 16,000'; no doubt an exaggerated figure since he would not have had time for other duties. Not content with these high-handed proceedings Coke compelled them 'under most grievous penalties to give bail for their good behaviour'. Aside from the financial losses to Catholics there was also the incalculable damage done to communities and families by the activities of pursuivants who inspired a culture of fear. That they were highly effective in ferreting out suspected Catholics is clear from the numerous complaints made about them in the letters and reports of the missionaries. 'The pursuivants, by apprehending priests and catholics, are grown so rich that they hire spies to serve their turn, in so much as there is not a host, chamberlain, or ostler which is not ready to inform them of the behaviour of their guests. If they see a man modest and civil, it is enough to set the pursuivant upon him.'[9]

TWELVE

Postlude: The Plot and the Playwright

The public theatres of Elizabethan London were built and occupied for one over-riding purpose – to offer varied entertainment to those who would pay for it. So much is clear, but it scampers over the question of why within a generation of the first openings in the 1570s the city had more of these private enterprises than any other place in Europe. One reason may have been that they offered a notable variety of new drama and hence drew a very large, variously responsive, mixed public audience hankering for novelty and diversion. 'No longer subject to the propagandistic requirements of pre-Elizabethan factionalism, the companies now found that professionalism was replacing partisanship as the crucial virtue of their trade.'[1] Privy councillors tolerated the public theatre because it provided a useful testing-ground for court entertainment, and of course sometimes it was literally necessary to divert Elizabeth from some self-inflicted policy absurdity. What worries they had were (for the most part) about public order and public health. The city fathers had rather more to consider and their opposition was a significant factor in the development of the theatre during the last quarter of the century. They had a particular fretting concern that people at the playhouse by day were not working productively, and since a capacity house at the Red Bull in Clerkenwell was some three thousand spectators, and it was only one of a large cluster, this notion is not entirely risible.[2] Lurid stories and instances of sin at the playhouse also perturbed them, and some held that playing incurred the wrath of God.

Both court and city regulators could also be troubled by the rapid development of a coincidence between the language of poetry and that of the law and politics. In theatres it became possible to give vent to matters of public concern, or controversy – which had in some measure been the situation before Elizabeth's accession. In that tense and difficult period between the Henrician sundering of the connection with Rome and the consolidation of Protestant power under Elizabeth players often got to present one view or another in the religious controversy.[3] The way in which late Elizabethan and Jacobean playwrights took on matters of public concern can confuse us today, just as it may have done their immediate audiences. But what a succulent bait controversy can be, especially when there were views to be formed in retrospect of the late queen and prospect of the new king. An example would be Thomas Dekker's political pageant *The Whore of Babylon* (1607), which hailed the towering virtues of Elizabeth and vituperatively condemned the 'continual bloody stratagems, of that Purple whore of Rome'. In this allegorical celebration of past but memorable Elizabethan triumphs there is only one allusion to James couched in flattering terms. Yet this alone has suggested to some commentators that the play was a pro-Jacobean piece written to chime with the collective sigh of relief in the country for the failure of the gunpowder plot.[4] Even so, unlike his predecessor, James had negotiated peace in 1604 with the great and still hated enemy, while in the aftermath of the plot Salisbury had carefully modified the severity once exhibited by his own father in the aftermath of the rebellion of the northern earls. This time the Secretary narrowed the focus of retribution to plotters and remoter Jesuits whom he could not reach without covert efforts. So praise of Elizabeth by Dekker, the idealization of her legacy, lends itself to the view that the play is a disguised criticism of the milder Jacobean way. The 'political valence' of such plays is decidedly wobbly, and in addition it is almost impossible to ascertain the level of attention and response of an audience then.

As Elizabeth aged in the 1590s the charmed ruthlessness of her coercion and that of her greybeard council tended to fade; the demand for docility from her subjects was a mite less insistent. Voices of criticism were heard, isolated by a heftier deference for the time being, but plain enough in the House of Commons, and too the theatres, to draw rebuke. The 'public stage [then] was the freest open forum for political speculation', and not even the furtive presence of intelligencers could stifle it entirely. So the playwrights were freer than members of the House of Commons to initiate a debate, even if it was rather halting and never went very far. Peter Wentworth, the Protestant parliamentarian, died in prison in 1597 for promoting the claim of James VI to the English throne. That year too Thomas Nashe and Ben Jonson co-authored the (lost) comedy *The Isle of Dogs*, which irked someone at court because it satirized the queen's courtiers, yet in contrast to Wentworth the playwrights were only lightly punished. The play was, of course, suppressed, the playwrights in some measure chastised – then the affront was forgotten because the theatre had no palpable authority.[5] It was a consumer-driven forum and the powerlessness of the stage virtually guaranteed the actors and theatre entrepreneurs a marked prosperity if they could perform as often as possible. The key to this was public health and the virulence of the plague. For the most part government censorship over the stage was inconsistent and rather mildly permissive in the treatment of topical matters. The Master of the Revels, a court appointee, had a remarkably light hand in this respect, as well as a financial interest of his own in the well-being of the companies; they paid him to approve performances. There was therefore no royal whim of iron in dealing with playwrights and acting companies by 1600; they were regarded as individuals working for a living. Neither Shakespeare nor the Lord Chamberlain's players at the Globe, who had been paid to re-stage his play *Richard II* for the Essex conspirators in February 1601, were a whit worse off for having hired out their space, time and skills in performance.

The headlong enthusiasm and wild failings of such men in public and private matters did not alter Shakespeare's admiration for aristocracy in general and the Earl of Southampton in particular (the earl being himself an ardent supporter of

Essex). Southampton had been Shakespeare's patron years before, and if the gunpowder plot had succeeded, he and another aristocrat who figured importantly in the playwright's life, William Herbert, Earl of Pembroke, would have been killed in the massacre that was projected. The deep purpose of the plot was then rather blurred and variously conceived, but there was widespread suspicion that the Earl of Northumberland, ninth in line of succession before James arrived to take the throne, was discontented, would have benefited from the plot and therefore was involved. Unlike the late Christopher Marlowe and also John Donne, who remarkably in February 1602 had been able to use Northumberland to deliver the letter that told Sir George More that his daughter was secretly married to the poet, Shakespeare was not of the earl's Syon House coterie of brilliant intellectuals.[6] So did he know, for example, that in July 1604, after Southampton had offended the king, that it was Northumberland who had delivered the response of the privy council? It would have been a difficult encounter between the two grandees because some years before there had been talk of a duel between them and the animosity remained. Northumberland was certainly capable of nursing a grudge, and proved it when before the king and court he spat into Sir Francis Vere's face. This dismal incident led to his banishment to the Archbishop of Canterbury's summer home in Croydon.

Even before he began work on *Macbeth*, Shakespeare seems to have regarded the long line of the Percy family with disapproval and his use of their rebellions as plot material in the Henry IV plays is well known and has been analysed elsewhere.[7] The exasperated Hotspur in them certainly bears a neatly identified vocal link in his stutter to the then current earl, and it may be that in *Macbeth* he was insinuating to an alert audience that Northumberland, despite his vehement denials, had indeed been involved in the gunpowder plot. It was, after all, common knowledge that Beaumont, the French ambassador who had so frantically quit the country then, had been a close friend of the earl. Was it a royal commission, as some critics have averred, that set Shakespeare to work on *Macbeth*? For this there is no evidence and a number of things militate against it. The most emphatic must be that James had no sustained interest in drama; plays were put on at court for festivities and quite often he was absent, though Queen Anne and Prince Henry would join the audience. Secondly, if Shakespeare had wanted to please the monarch there were certainly other topics from Scottish history he could have worked up into a satisfactory offering. Instead his darting imagination was seized by an event which if it had succeeded could have pitched the country into years of turbulence and random bloodshed. To many people the plot was the atrocious climax of years of clandestine effort; in both England and Scotland the threat to the legitimate ruler had been great. In the play evil ambition is viewed as a destructive abomination, just the view taken by Bishop Andrewes in his plot sermons afterwards. Divine providence, as it seemed, had saved James in 1600 from the Gowrie conspiracy and then again had stalled mayhem in 1605 to save the nation from calamity. These two events were of immense interest, and the second tended to enhance interest in the first so that Shakespeare had a rare opportunity to write a play that chimed with the topical, eyeing an event that had an intense whiff of the local for him in Stratford.[8]

It is assumed that he was not in London as the turbulence over the plot swept the city then the country, and everyone nervously peered at their neighbourhood for signs of insurrection. For example, Richard Jones saw Sir Francis Smythe ride out of London on the 4th and return on Thursday week, 'when it should seem he had ridden very hard, for the Wednesday following his horse was so weary that he could not rise when Jones kicked him as he lay in the stable at the Red Lion, Holborn'. Shakespeare may have been still in Oxford, or more likely Stratford by then, but with the reopening of the theatres on 15 December he would surely have come back to London and he encountered in the cold and gloom of the winter city an additional burden on the spirits, a doom–laden distress and shock which took months to dissipate. The successful theatre manager and playwright had never written a play set in the London of his day, and again he chose not to do so. Instead he set to reading background material for a Scottish play that would be for his public a mordant commentary on the lure of kingship and the wretched perversities it could induce within hitherto worthwhile men – a lure that had once or twice led James himself into some ill-conceived acts of policy while fretting away the time before Elizabeth died. There were some risks in writing a conspiracy play as Ben Jonson had found with *Sejanus* (1603), and anything bearing on such activity as well as on Scottish matters was bound to be scrutinized by the government in one guise or another. Such had been the case a few years before as Shakespeare would have been well aware. On the fourth anniversary of the Gowrie conspiracy, when the Ruthven brothers had reportedly sought to murder James, the King's Servants (once the Lord Chamberlain's Men) intended to perform a play (now lost) based on that intriguing and never fully explained hubbub at Gowrie House, near Perth. Prior to this play by an unnamed author (or authors) the official version of the event had been a pamphlet published in Scotland and then reprinted in London late in 1600. The Master of the Revels allowed the play for performance, and it attracted a good deal of interest, being 'twice represented . . . with exceeding concourse of all sorts of people'. Then it was suppressed with the excuse that some men in government felt it was unseemly to present princes on stage in their own lifetime. Such a lame stipulation had not been invoked a decade before when Marlowe's *The Massacre of Paris*, with equivalent staged horrors, had played at the Rose very successfully.[9]

So, who were the 'great Councillors' who objected to the Gowrie play? Northampton perhaps, Robert Cecil probably and most likely Thomas Sackville, Earl of Dorset, who many years before had been the co-author of *Gorboduc*, the first English blank verse tragedy that had influenced Shakespeare's writing of *King Lear* in 1605. As Chancellor of Oxford University, Dorset was formally responsible for entertaining the great royal cavalcade headed by James when it descended on the town in late August. A number of plays were put on, including the playlet by Matthew Gwinne, *Tre Quasi Sibyllae*, acted by students which 'recast the legendary threefold prophecy given to Macbeth as a threefold compliment to James'.[10] It is not clear if the King's Servants were there, or whether they had been excluded deliberately as a rebuke for the misliked Gowrie play. It remains a distinct possibility that it was Dorset who conveyed to the Globe's house playwright that a suitable subject for a play on a Scottish theme might be found in the chroniclers. And can there be much doubt that the company would have wanted a new play with a satisfactory appeal to a king who preferred sitting in the saddle to sitting watching actors? The public audience, revelling in correspondences, still hugely curious about their new monarch and his background, was certain to flock to it. So Shakespeare had a commercial imperative, especially since the playhouse seasons were being so frequently disrupted by the plague. His company did have some fence building to do with James, but this does not make *Macbeth* a calculated piece of gross flattery and 'the play's acclaim of the king's safe reign, if that, is at best only modestly expressed'.

The task before Shakespeare was the tricky one of writing a unified historical drama using material familiar to the court and its denizens, but simultaneously making it a public-grabbing shocker. This dual aspect of the play is constantly rehearsed in the language with the frequent use of the word 'double' and a rich scattering of other words of that sense.[11] Even 'double' itself comes twice with the witches' 'Double, double' in the cauldron scene. The play doubles violence, swerving between its demonization and the 'contemplation of violent solutions to the historical blockages and depredations that form its core'. Macbeth tries to 'make assurance double sure', as did the Gowries in 1582 and 1600, and the gunpowder plotters did with their two-pronged attempt to sweep away much of the ruling class in London and the Midlands. Perhaps we can even say that Shakespeare, not being content with his reading on Scottish history in the accounts printed by Raphael Holinshed, had doubled back (so to speak) to the Gowrie play/plot to give weight and historical density to a more remote story. The official account of the plot supplied him with extra details which he then projected backwards and forwards; for example, the dagger omitted in the historical sources 'is quite as central to the Gowrie account as it is to Macbeth'. The late Leslie Hotson was briskly certain that Shakespeare did not model his characters directly on contemporaries but gossipy old John Aubrey knew better and there seems to be a very strong likelihood that the Thane of Cawdor in the play, who betrays King Duncan, and is executed, was based on both the former Earl of Gowrie, an open rebel, and Sir Everard Digby. When the latter was executed Shakespeare was lodging a short walk away from St Paul's and might easily have strolled there to observe the grisly business before writing scene IV in Act One. As it was, Digby and Robert Catesby were held to be handsome men; a double helping of good looks. But 'Fair is foul, and foul is fair,' the witches chant together at the beginning of the act to nudge the audience so that even the sleepiest pitling knew that as ever he should be ready for dramatic reversals. Shakespeare obviously meant the play to wrap up aspects of contemporary events, revising them unexpectedly, and Act II Scene III, the notorious porter scene, certainly does this with the 3 May 1606 execution of Father Garnet.

As it has been shown (see Chapter 9) Garnet's dogged defence of equivocation had thrust that specialized doctrine into the forefront of public consciousness. When the porter jeeringly reckons he has an equivocator knocking for entry, the audience knew that Garnet was being mocked; a man who had committed 'treason enough for God's sake', but had then failed to enter Heaven and now solicits entry at what doubles as hell-gate and the entrance to Inverness castle. Even those in the undoubtedly gleeful audience who had missed his trial and execution now got a second opportunity to holler and deride him. What the porter has to say as he lumbers about contains a clutch of sly references intended to stir them: 'Here's a farmer that hanged himself on the expectation of plenty' threads together two jokes. It occasioned two guffaws here because it was widely known that Garnet had on occasions used the pseudonym Farmer, and because market speculation in the price of grain was a matter of consuming interest to townspeople buying bread as their staple food. In fact, the hopes of a good harvest were abundantly fulfilled in 1606, but there was no subsequent drop in price, so any farmer behaving so had fatally miscalculated (like Farmer). Scarcity abroad caused a rise not a fall in grain prices, a matter which troubled Zorzi Giustinian in August when he entered the market to buy corn (as he called it) for export to Venice.[12]

The scene begins with punning on proper names: 'If a man were porter of hell-gate, he should have old turning the key.' The other Jesuit arrested with Garnet at Hindlip was Father Old/corne, and Robert Keyes was in the second rank of conspirators. Some years ago an interesting (albeit not totally convincing) suggestion was made for the identity of the porter himself who finds his workplace too cold for hell. It was that he was an audience-teasing (mis)representation of Guy Fawkes, so frequently referred to then as 'the devil', 'the chief devil' and 'the devil in the vault'.[13] The identification could have been played up even then by judicious use of a prop lantern like that supposedly found when Fawkes was seized, which is now in the Ashmolean Museum, Oxford. Could the porter's very deliberate response to the

The authenticity of this lantern in the Ashmolean Museum, Oxford, has not gone unchallenged. If it did not belong to Fawkes no doubt he used one very like it

repeated knocking of the blameless Macduff and Lennox have a double meaning? First, as a parody of Fawkes's apparently sluggish response to the government searches of 4/5 November; and second, as a parody of the gate keeper of Blackfriars, the London home of the Earl of Northumberland. When he does eventually open the gate the porter has a series of punning jokes on the effects of drink, 'an equivocator with lechery', such as Garnet was said to have been by his enemies in his dealings with Anne Vaux. His last lines are all about hanging, the words indicating a laugh being 'throat', 'legs' and 'shift', this latter the post-mortem garment of the hanged man. So the meanings pile up.

As do the dates for the inception, writing, completion and first performance of the play. One recent revisionist view is that it was written in the latter half of 1603 in the aftermath of the Bye plot. But that episode, tiresome as it was for the government, had none of the resonance of the Gowrie plot which from 1603–5 was marked in England as a national holiday; nor of the gunpowder plot which for many months stupefied the nation. Both became 'political' festivals, with the latter having a far more extended hold on the collective memory. This was because the personnel, and very buildings of government, some very old and saturated with history, had been threatened. The succession too was dangerously jeopardized with the first royal family for over fifty years in peril. Most commentators on *Macbeth* see signs of haste in it, and the hurry according to one was not simply commercial, but the need to finish the play several weeks before a 7 August 1606 performance by the King's Servants before James and his brother-in-law King Christian IV of Denmark.[14] But there is no record of such a performance, even of the play in an abbreviated form for a royal audience that liked short plays before long ones. Yet this absence is not conclusive either, because the company records are not complete. There is also the counter suggestion that the porter's third would-be entrant through hell-gate, 'an English tailor', refers to a matter of some public notoriety that occurred later in the year. Hugh Griffin was just such an English tailor (albeit suspiciously Welsh-sounding) who became famous in November-December for his part in the so-called miracle of Father Garnet's straw. This was a head of straw drenched with Garnet's blood from his dismemberment and obtained by a young Catholic, John Wilkinson, who took it to Griffin's house. Some time later the pious householder noticed that the blood as it seemed to him had dried in such a way on one of the husks as to form a small but accurate image of Garnet's own features. Since he was a martyr in Catholic eyes such an item fast became an object of wonder and veneration. Late in November, and again early in December, Griffin was examined by the Archbishop of Canterbury. By 1610 Garnet's straw was familiar to Europeans like Andreas Eudaemon-Joannes who had it rendered as an engraved illustration for his *Apologia* for the late Jesuit. If Shakespeare intended this snippet of the porter scene to deride Catholic illusions and it was written at the same time as the rest, not worked in later, then it becomes doubtful if *Macbeth* was completed before early 1607.[15] This would put the first public performance in April because again the plague seems to have closed the theatres from January to March 1608. Performances there must have been if the echoes of *Macbeth* in other plays through 1607 are accepted. One possibility is of public performances following a full-length court performance during the Christmas festivities of December 1606–January 1607. That brief period seems to have been especially rich, with performances of *Antony and Cleopatra* and *King Lear*, although the writing order was surely *Lear, Antony and Cleopatra* and *Macbeth*.

Shakespeare's career was never troubled by incarceration in the way that Ben Jonson's was. He was without the confrontational element in his personality, agreeing to marry an older woman, but then opting to leave her for long periods while she raised his children. Jonson, on the other hand, was a brawler, and not inclined to ingratiate himself with audiences, so that his own efforts at conspiracy drama, dressing them in togas, were dismal failures; *Catiline* was famously hissed from the stage even if it did deploy aspects of the gunpowder plot. Yet Shakespeare did create a problem of writing decorum for himself by 'following the action primarily through the consciousness of Macbeth himself'. This hauled the playwright to the brink of human, if not moral ambiguity, so while he and his audience recognize evil in the ambition to murder a king and supplant his royal line, by trailing the regicide through his torrent of crimes, including infanticide, his suffering too in the ghastly sequence becomes apparent. For the richer, better placed gentlemen like Rookwood and Digby joining the gunpowder plot became a calamitous exercise in self-destruction, requiring them simultaneously to squander their wealth and suppress their duty and affection for king, wives and children. Macbeth and Robert Catesby command loyalty from their followers even though what they envisage and in some measure carry out is savagely delinquent. There was a curious knot of blood between the imagined regicide, the imagination of a would-be regicide and the Gowries. The first suspicion of responsibility for killing Duncan falls on two unfortunate grooms killed by Macbeth before they can give testimony in their own defence. This accelerated despatch was also the fate of Alexander Ruthven and his brother, the Earl of Gowrie, in 1600, and then Thomas Percy and Catesby in 1605. So strange and unnecessary did this seem then that many suspected the government of a deliberate act of manipulation to eliminate them without trial. Indeed, such was the swell of incredulity then that it was thought necessary to make a public explanation of why Percy had not been taken alive; the claim was the familiar one of over-zealous subordinates wrecking matters. There was also the bizarre manner in which Catesby and Percy had died – the reports said one shot had despatched them – actually two balls from the same musket. A Catholic source recorded that the John Streete who achieved this odd feat stepped out from behind a tree to fire it.[16] For Shakespeare the ambush from one tree was too small for a grand climax and it grows dramatically to become Birnam Wood. Catesby suffered a retribution appropriate for history, while that for Macbeth suits the theatre. But what did Catholics in Yorkshire make of the play when it was given, apparently in the shortened memorial reconstruction of the 1608 quarto, by Sir Richard Cholmeley's players at Candlemas 1610 at Crowthwaite Hall – home of the recusant Yorke family?

Every year after the gunpowder plot the day was marked by the ringing of church bells, the lighting of bonfires, and special sermons in churches across the land. It was not a holiday as such, but certainly special, an occasion to reflect on God's providence and his mercies to England. Published on 5 November 1605 Sir Francis Bacon's *Advancement of Learning* declared, 'This Kingdom of England, having Scotland united, and shipping maintained, is one of the greatest monarchies that hath been in the world.' Since Bacon himself was straining after advancement the fraudulent exaggeration was understandable, but the twist in the sentence was not very well judged. He was blatantly rejigging very recent history. Of course it was true that for hundreds of years it had been the aim of the English kings and their supporters to unite the whole island of Britain in a federation. Where Edward I had failed, James had been allowed to succeed, yet not every Englishman was pleased or contented, and there was stubborn resistance within Parliament and without to the Union that James desired. Shakespeare was more subtle than Bacon; in *Macbeth* he finds an English slant though this is his Scottish play, for when Macbeth has done his worst the hope for the future is a Scottish prince, who comes out of England's protective embrace. With art that conceals the playwright gently misleads those who give such things superficial attention. He does this first by making King Duncan a saintly and paternal character (James saw himself as the unique progenitor of his united kingdom). But in the sources for the play Duncan was criticized and George Buchanan (once tutor to James) described the earlier monarch being 'of more indulgence to his own kindred than became a king'. Holinshed thought the same 'how negligent he was in punishing offenders'. The consequence was 'manic mis-ruled persons took occasion thereof to trouble the peace and quiet state of the commonwealth, by seditious commotions.' Shakespeare had enough distance from the affairs of state to nod in wry agreement when he read this. And he could further slide together for comparison the past and present by reflecting on the king's son.[17]

The chronicles made Malcolm into the ideal king with soaring praise, his natural piety strengthened by marriage to an English princess who was later canonized. He was described as taking great pains to amend the public manners of his kingdom, setting an example that inspired others 'to a Modest, Just and Sober life'. On reflection how very different from the sometimes unseemly exhibitions of James, whose piety was of the learned, bookish sort, who was far from modest in public or private matters and who frequently drank beyond the dictates of thirst. For an example of ill-regarded boorish behaviour Shakespeare had the shameless royal competitive drinking that took place when Christian IV and his brother-in-law visited Salisbury's great country mansion Theobalds late in July 1606 when the avenues to the house were strewn with gold oak leaves inscribed 'Welcome'. Then the masque devised by Ben Jonson and Inigo Jones stumbled into a bacchic rout because vice got the controlling hand and all the performers were riotously drunk. By contrast, the strong reputation for orderly behaviour, good sense and sobriety that attached to Prince Henry, held out promise for the future. So when William Leigh preached to his parishioners at Standish in Lancashire on the first anniversary of the gunpowder plot, 'Great Britaines Great Deliverance from the Great Danger of Popish Powder' was dedicated to Prince Henry.[18] One of the covert implications of *Macbeth* for a metropolitan audience was that whatever disaster threatened the kingdom a young ruler was in the making whose careful exercise of divinely granted authority would achieve a sound balance between slackness and raging brutality. It seemed to many that God had intervened on 5 November to prevent a change from the former to the latter – 'through God's mercy the change was prevented: the change of a noble Kingdom into an anarchy and Babylonian tyranny.'

Appendix I

THE GUNPOWDER COMMEMORATIVE PAINTING IN NEW COLLEGE, OXFORD

This picture curiosity which derides the plotters showing Justitia passing through a triumphal arch, and lauds the royal family, remains comparatively little known despite the article (already cited) by G. Wickham Legg. An error in this was corrected in 1986 by Professor Höltgen when he pointed out that a somewhat fleshy blond figure is a personification of Divine Bounty: *Bonitas Divina*, not a clumsy and ambiguous rendering of God.[1] Most recently work has been done on the picture by Ralph Weller, in his research for a study of the picture's donor, Dr Richard Haydocke (1569–1642/3).[2] Although Haydocke was himself a painter and engraver, as well as a physician and translator, the work in question was executed by John Percivall. He came from a family of minor artists working in Salisbury in the first half of the seventeenth century. The town commissioned several copies of original portraits of Charles I and his queen, as well as of William Herbert, 3rd Earl of Pembroke, for many years Salisbury's High Steward, and Percivall very likely worked from portraits in Wilton House where the Percivall family had worked as gilders.

The gunpowder painting is also a copy of an allegorical engraving done for the seventh anniversary of the plot in 1612. Because Prince Henry died on 6 November that year, the print was swiftly withdrawn from sale, when only a very few copies had been bought by courtiers such as Pembroke. Nearly seventy years later, at the time of the commotion caused by Titus Oates, the anti-Catholic engraving was reissued by Richard Northcott of Cornhill. From a unique copy, formerly in the collection of the Marquess of Bute, and now in the Huntington Library, California, it is possible to see that the print varies from the painting in only three ways:

(a)   Most of the inscriptions and mottoes in the painting are in Latin, while the versions in the print are in English.

(b)   The tablet on the extreme right-hand of the picture celebrates in Latin in the painting Haydocke's connection with his former college. In the print there is a snatch of verse in English and a quotation from Psalms.

(c)   At the foot of the painting are nine stanzas in Latin and a Latin scriptural quotation within a roundel. The print has ten stanzas of English verse.

This allegorical engraving, first issued in 1612 and again in about 1679, when anti-papist agitation by Titus Oates was rife, was used for a painting by a provincial artist, John Percivall. The painting is now in New College, Oxford. (Reproduced by permission of The Huntington Library, San Marino, California)

The other variation was in size – the painting being almost exactly twice the size of the engraving (3ft 4½ in × 2ft 8½ in against 19½ in × 14 in). As Ralph Weller noted in a private letter, an experienced engraver like Haydocke would have found it a simple task to 'square up' the canvas and define the general outline of the picture for Percivall by doubling dimensions taken from the print's first issues.

Some work still remains to be done on the musical notation in the painting, and a start on this has been made by a graduate student of New College, Timothy Morris. For the origins of the music I suggested a crypto-Catholic composer, but as he pointed out in a private letter, the open book in the top right of the painting shows a Magnificat, and this suggests an Anglican, not a Catholic origin 'since evensong had become the principal focus of Protestant musicians' attention'. He suggested too that the music came either from Oxford or Cambridge, or possibly the Chapel Royal, which had always had the privilege (like the universities) of using Latin for its services.

Appendix II

THE SWORDS OF THE GENTLEMEN

On Wednesday 6 November 1605 a London cutler, John Cradock, made a statement to the embattled Lord Chief Justice, Sir John Popham. In it Cradock outlined how he had been initially employed by the plotter Ambrose Rookwood to do work embellishing a special sword. During the summer of that year the wealthy young man had commissioned him to put a Spanish blade into a sword hilt that was itself unusual because it showed the story of the Passion of Christ in ornamental plaques. Cradock described these as 'richly engraved' – the meaning then being that they were low relief items. Since swords (rapiers) were worn by all gentlemen in public such insistent imagery was likely to cause comment when it was noted and was 'a potentially dangerous statement of faith'.[1] Rookwood evidently had an appetite for conspicuous display, and just a few days before the 'dire combustion' he changed his mind about the handle or grip. Cradock was told to remove it and replace it with a gold one before joining it to the hilt. The finished sword was then discreetly delivered to Rookwood at his London lodgings on the Sunday night at 11 o'clock. A further delivery of a less grandly decorated sword was then made to Thomas Winter, staying at an inn in the Strand just beyond the well-known premises of Mr Patrick. Winter had paid £12 10s. four months before on commissioning the work. Thomas Percy had also ordered one at slightly less cost, paying 10s. down towards the final price of £7, but he never got to collect it and Cradock held the sword at his premises. As expert consultant on these purchases Christopher Wright, one of the leading swordsmen of the day, went to the shop to give an appraisal of the blade length and so on. Rookwood was clearly wealthy, and could afford to indulge an expensive whim, spending £19 10s. – the price noted by Popham in a letter to Salisbury written before the interrogation of the cutler. The additional work may have boosted the price beyond the £20 mark; a princely sum at that time for a sword, as the other examples cited by Claude Blair in his recent article indicate.[2]

So Rookwood had a sword which in its decoration was laden with Catholic symbolism. It is doubtful if it or the others prepared were ever used, even in the final stand at Holbeach, since by then the plotters had a great stock of utilitarian weaponry to hand. When they were killed (like Thomas Percy and Christopher Wright) items of value about their bodies were apparently looted for private gain.

A number of the plotters were regarded as first class swordsmen. Did this fine and very rare example belong to Thomas Percy? (Swiss National Museum, Zurich, LM3675)

When the plotters were injured and captured (like Rookwood and Winter) such things should have been seized and accounted for by their captors for presentation to the authorities in London. An item as rich as Rookwood's sword was evidently too great a temptation to someone in the raiding party. Perhaps the sheriff of Worcestershire saw it as his reward for a dangerous mission accomplished. Indeed, given the notable quality of the weapons, it is not entirely surprising that they were filched, but it is curious (and unsatisfactory) that as time passed, and presumably the swords were handed down through families, that they did not eventually surface in known collections. Were they perhaps broken up during the Civil War?

Today the Swiss National Museum in Zurich has the only sword (LM3675) that uniquely conforms to the description given by Cradock of his work.[3] This fine weapon, however, has an Ottoman blade and so cannot be assigned to Rookwood. The source of the scenes on the plaques, all reflecting Christ's suffering from the Betrayal to the Crucifixion, has not yet been identified, but perhaps the artist was Wierix who later engraved a portrait medallion of Fr. Henry Garnet. Since John Cradock, cutler, had not been paid in full for the sword set up for Thomas Percy, he was probably allowed to keep it. Cradock was himself

a Catholic and it may be that he held on to the sword before later allowing it to pass by sale or gift into fraternal Catholic hands – like Sir Charles or Sir Allan Percy. How it came so much later into Swiss hands remains a mystery since the family anecdote is clearly wrong. Cradock himself remains, too, something of a mystery because the early records of the London Cutlers' Company are incomplete. Given that the plotters were so often in the Strand, it is no surprise that they went to him since he was living, according to the poor-rate books of the parish of St Clement's Dane, at Temple Bar in the Strand. He remained there, probably as a working cutler rather than simply a retailer, until 1610 when he seems to have retired to the nearby parish of St Giles in the Field. His will, undated but proved in 1623, shows him to have been a well-off property owner despite his recusant status.[4]

Abbreviations

APC	Acts of the Privy Council
BIHR	*Bulletin of the Institute of Historical Research*
BL	British Library
CHR	*Catholic Historical Review*
CRS	*Catholic Record Society*
CSPD	*Calendar of State Papers, Domestic*
CSPV	*Calendar of State Papers, Venetian*
EHR	*English History Review*
ELH	*English Literary History*
ELR	*English Literary Renaissance*
HT	*History Today*
JBS	*Journal of British Studies*
JMRS	*Journal of Medieval and Renaissance Studies*
JRA	*Journal of the Royal Artillery*
N & Q	*Notes and Queries*
NCE	*New Civil Engineer*
NPP	*Northamptonshire Past and Present*
P & P	*Past and Present*
PMLA	*Publications of the Modern Language Association*
PRO	Public Record Office
RES	*Review of English Studies*
RH	*Recusant History*
RHS	*Royal Historical Society*
RUS	*Rice University Studies*
Sh Q	*Shakespeare Quarterly*
Sh S	*Shakespeare Studies*
TAPS	*Transactions of the American Philosophical Society*
TBMI	*Transactions of the Birmingham and Midland Institute*
TMBS	*Transactions of the Monumental Brass Society*
TRHS	*Transactions of the Royal Historical Society*
TSC	*The Seventeenth Century*
WR	*World Review*

Bibliography

PRIMARY SOURCES

BL   Additional Mss
BL   Harleian Mss
BL   Lansdowne Mss

Acts of the Privy Council (new series)
Akrigg, G.P.V. (ed.), *Letters of King James VI & I*, 1983.
Barlow, T. (ed.), *The Gunpowder Treason*, 1679.
Birch, T., *The Court and Times of James I*, (ed.) P. Williams, Vol. I, 1849.
Calendar of State Papers, Domestic.
Calendar of State Papers, Venetian.
Caraman, P. (ed.), *John Gerard, The Autobiography of an Elizabethan*, 1956.
Edwards, F. (ed.), *The Gunpowder Plot: The Narrative of Oswald Tesimond, alias Greenway*, 1973.
Kingdon, R.M. (ed.), *William Cecil; The Execution of Justice in England*, 1583, reprinted New York, 1965.
Stephens, E., *Popish Policies . . .*, 1674.
Verstegen, R. (also Robert Persons), *A Conference about the Next Succession*, 1594, reprinted London, 1972.

SECONDARY SOURCES

Anstruther, G., *Vaux of Harrowden; A Recusant Family*, 1953.
Archer, J.M., *Sovereignty and Intelligence, Spying and Court Culture in the English Renaissance*, 1993.
Aveling, H., *Northern Catholics*, 1970.
Axton, M., 'The Queen's Two Bodies; Drama and the Elizabethan Succession', *RHS*, 1977.
Belloc, H., *A History of England*, Vol. 4, 1925–31.
Bossy, J., *The English Catholic Community, 1570–1850*, 1976.
Brodrick, J., *The Life and Work of Blessed Robert Francis*, 1928.
Caraman, P., *Henry Garnet, 1555–1606, and the Gunpowder Plot*, 1964.
Cecil, A., *A Life of Robert Cecil, 1st Earl of Salisbury*, 1915.
Clancy, T., *Papist Pamphleteers, The Allen-Persons party and the political thought of the Counter-Reformation in England, 1572–1615*, Chicago, 1964.
Collinson, P., *The Religion of Protestants, the Church in English Society, 1559–1625*, 1982.
Cressy, D., *Bells and Bonfires; National memory and the Protestant calendar in Elizabethan and Stuart England*, 1989.
Davidson, C., *The Primrose Way*, 1970.
Davies, R., *The Fawkes's of York in the Sixteenth Century*, 1850.
De Luna, B., *Jonson's Romish Plot; A Study of* Catiline *and its historical context*, 1967.

Dixon, W.H., *Her Majesty's Tower*, 2 vols, 1885.

Durst, P., *Intended Treason; What really happened in the Gunpowder Plot*, 1970.

Edwards, F., *Guy Fawkes; The Real Story of the Gunpowder Plot?*, 1969.

Gallagher, L., *Medusa's Gaze, Casuistry and Conscience in the Renaissance*, 1991.

Galloway, B., *The Union of England and Scotland, 1603–8*, Edinburgh, 1986.

Gardiner, S.R., *What Gunpowder Plot was*, 1897.

Gerard, J., *What was the Gunpowder Plot*, 1897.

Guiney, L., *Recusant Poets*, 1938.

Hales, J.W., *Notes and Essays*, 1884.

Handover, P.M., *The Second Cecil, The Rise to Power, 1563–1604 of Sir Robert Cecil*, 1959.

Haynes, A., *Robert Cecil, 1st Earl of Salisbury; Servant of Two Sovereigns*, 1989.

—— *Invisible Power; The Elizabethan Secret Services, c. 1570–1603*, 1992.

Henderson, T.F., *James I & VI*, 2 vols, 1904.

Henry, G., *The Irish Military Community in Spanish Flanders, 1586–1621*, Dublin, 1992.

Holmes, P., *Resistance and Compromise, The Political Thought of the Elizabethan Catholics*, 1982.

Hotson, J.L., *I, William Shakespeare*, 1937.

Hughes, P., *Rome and the Counter-Reformation*, 1942.

Hurstfield, J., *Freedom, Corruption and Government in Elizabethan England*, 1973.

Janelle, P., *Robert Southwell*, 1935.

Jardine, D., *A Narrative of the Gunpowder Plot*, 1857.

Jessopp, A., *John Donne*, 1891.

—— *Letters of Father H. Walpole*, 1873.

Jones, M.W., *The Gunpowder Plot*, 1909.

Lee (Jnr), M., *Great Britain's Solomon; James VI & I in his three Kingdoms* (Champaign, Ill.), 1990.

Leites, E., *Conscience and Casuistry in Early Modern Europe*, 1988.

Lindley, D. & Sowerby, R. (eds), *Thomas Campion 'De pulverea coniuratione'*, Leeds Texts and Monographs, ns, 10 (Leeds), 1987.

Longueville, T., *The Life of a Conspirator*, 1895.

Loomie, A.J., *The Spanish Elizabethans; the English Exiles at the Court of Philip II*, 1965.

—— 'Spain and the Jacobean Catholics', *CRS*, Records series, Vol. 64, 1973.

Lossky, N., *Lancelot Andrewes, The Preacher, The Origins of the Mystical Theology of the Church of England*, 1991.

Magee, B., *The English Recusants*, 1938.

Mathew, D., *Catholicism in England, the portrait of a minority, its culture and traditions*, 1955.

—— *The Celtic Peoples and Renaissance Europe*, 1933.

Mathias, R., *Whitsun Riot*, 1963.

McIlwain, C., *The Political Works of James I*, 1918.

Milward, P., *Shakespeare's Religious Background*, 1973.

Morgan, G.B., *The Great English Treason*, 2 vols, 1931–2.

Mutschmann, H., *Shakespeare and Catholicism*, 1952.

Nicholl, C., *The Reckoning; The Murder of Christopher Marlowe*, 1992.

Nicholls, M., *Investigating Gunpowder Plot*, 1991.

Nichols, S. & Robinson, F. (eds), *The Meaning of Mannerism*, 1972.

Ottley, R.L., *Lancelot Andrewes*, 1891.

Parish, J., 'Robert Parsons', *RUS*, Vol. 52, no 1, 1966.

Paul, H.N., *The Royal Play of Macbeth*, 1950.

Petersson, R.T., *Sir Kenelm Digby, The Ornament of England, 1603–65*, 1956.

Petti, A. (ed.), 'The Letters and Despatches of Richard Verstegen, c. 1550–1640', *CRS*, iii, 1959.

Pollen, J.H., *Father Henry Garnet and the Gunpowder Plot*, 1888.

Pye, C., *The Regal Phantasm*, 1990.

Reynolds, E., *Campion and Persons*, 1980.

Rombauts, E., *Richard Verstegen*, 1933.

Rose, E., *Cases of Conscience: Alternatives Open to Recusants and Puritans under Elizabeth I and James I*, 1979.

Ross, S., *History in hiding*, 1991.
Scoufos, A. L., *Shakespeare's Typological Satire*, 1979.
Sidney, Sir P., *A History of the Gunpowder Plot*, 1904.
Sisson, C.J., *Lost Plays of Shakespeare's Age*, 1936.
Slavin, A.J., 'The Precarious Balance', *Borzoi History of England*, 1973.
Smith, A.G.R. (ed.), *The Reign of James VI & I*, 1973.
Solt, L., *Church and State in Early Modern England*, 1990.
Spierenburg, P., *The Spectacle of Suffering*, 1984.
Spink, H.H., *The Gunpowder Plot and Lord Mounteagle's Letter*, 1902.
Stopes, C., *The Life of the 3rd Earl of Southampton*, 1922.
Storch, R., *Popular Culture and Custom*, 1982.
Trimble, W.R., *The Catholic Laity in Elizabethan England*, 1964.
Watkins, E.I., *Roman Catholicism in England from the Reformation*, 1957.
Williamson, H.R., *Four Stuart Portraits*, 1949.
—— *The Gunpowder Plot*, 1951.
Willson, D.H., *King James VI and I*, 1956.
Winstanley, L., *Macbeth, King Lear and Contemporary History*, 1922.

ARTICLES IN PERIODICALS

Anstruther, G., 'Powder Treason', *Blackfriars*, XXXIII, 1952.
Bossy, J., 'The Character of English Catholicism', *P & P*, 21, 1962.
Breight, C., '*The Tempest* and the Discourse of Treason', *Sh Q*, 41, 1, 1990.
Carrafiello, M., 'Robert Persons' Climate of Resistance and the Gunpowder Plot', *TSC*, 1988.
Dodd, A.H., 'The Spanish Treason, the Gunpowder Plot, and the Catholic Refugees', *EHR*, LIII, 1938.
Eccles, M., 'Jonson and the Spies', *RES*, XIII, 1937.
Edwards, F., 'Still Investigating Gunpowder Plot', *RH*, 21, 3, 1993.
Flynn, D., 'Donne and the Ancient Catholic Nobility', *ELR*, 19, 1989.
Hogg, O.F.G., 'Gunpowder and its Association with the Crown', *JRA*, LXXXI, 1944.
Hotine, M., 'Richard II and Macbeth – Studies in Tudor Tyranny', *N & Q*, ns. Vol. 38, 4, 1991.
Humphreys, J., 'The Wyntours of Huddington and the Gunpowder Plot', *TBMI*, XXX, 1904.
—— 'The Habingtons of Hindlip, and the Gunpowder Plot', *TBMI*, XXXI, 1905.
Huntley, F.L., '*Macbeth* and the background of Jesuitical Equivocation', *PMLA*, 79, 196.
Izon, J., 'New Light on the Gunpowder Plot', *HT*, IV, 1954.
Knipe, J., 'Conspiracy and conscience; A psychological study of the Gunpowder Plot', *TSC*, January/April 1930.
Kozikowski, S.J., 'The Gowrie Conspiracy against James VI; A new source for Shakespeare's Macbeth,' *Sh S*, XIII, 1980.
Legg, L.G., Wickham, 'On a Picture Commemorative', *Archaeologia*, 1934.
Loomie, A.J. (SJ), 'Toleration and Diplomacy', *TAPS*, 53 pt 6, 1963.
—— 'Guy Fawkes in Spain: The Spanish Treason in Spanish Documents', *BIHR*, Sp Supp 9, 1971.
Lunn, M., 'Chaplains to the English Regiment in Spanish Flanders', 1605–6', *RH*, XI, 19.
Nash, T.R., 'Copy of the original death-warrant of Humphrey Littleton', *Archaeologia*, XV, 1803.
Nicholls, M., 'Investigating Gunpowder Plot', *RH*, XIX, 1988.
Perry, 'Elizabeth in Jacobean London', *JMRS*, 23, 1, 1993.
Roger, N.A.M. (ed.), 'Ordnance Records and the Gunpowder Plot', *BIHR*, LIII, 1980.
Rogers, H.L., 'An English Tailor and Father Garnet's Straw', *RES*, ns, XVI, 1965.
Ryan, C.J., 'The Jacobean Oath of Allegiance and English Lay Catholics', *CHR*, XXVIII, 2, 1942.
Sprott, S.E., 'Sir Edmund Baynham', *RH*, X, 1964.
Stroud, T.A., 'Ben Jonson and Father Thomas Wright', *ELH*, 14, 4, 1947.
Stunz, A.N., 'The Date of Macbeth', *ELH*, IX, 1942.
Toyne, S.M., 'Guy Fawkes and the Powder Plot', *HT*, I, 1951.

Wake, J. (ed.), 'The Death of Francis Tresham, Northants', *P & P*, II, 1954.

Wiener, C.Z., 'The Beleaguered Isle: A Study of Elizabethan and Early Jacobean Anti-Catholicism, *P & P*, LI, 1971.

Williamson, H.R., 'The Gunpowder Plot', *WR*, November 1950.

Wilson, C.P.H., 'Monumental Brasses and the Gunpowder Plot', *TMBS*, 1972.

Wormald, J., 'Gunpowder, Treason and Scots', *JBS*, 24, 1985.

Yachnin, P., 'The Powerless Theatre' *ELR*, 21,1, 1991.

Notes

Chapter One

1 A.J. Slavin, 'The Precarious Balance' (*Borzoi History of England*, 1973), p. 286.
2 Ibid.
3 C.P.H. Wilson, 'Monumental Brasses and the Gunpowder Plot', *TMBS*, 1972, p. 268.
4 L. Solt, *Church and State in Early Modern England* (1990), p. 99.
5 Ibid., p. 101.
6 A.L. Rowse, *Eminent Elizabethans* (1983), pp. 42–73.
7 H. Trevor-Roper (Lord Dacre), *Historical Essays* (1957), pp. 42–73.
8 Solt, op. cit., p. 105.
9 B.W. Beckingsale, *Burghley: Tudor Statesman* (1967), p. 154.
10 D. Cressy, 'Binding the Nation: the Bonds of Association, 1584 and 1696'; in D.J. Gurth and J.W. McKenna (eds), *Tudor Rule and Revolution, Essays for G.R. Elton* (1982).
11 A. Haynes, *Invisible Power: The Elizabethan Secret Services* (1992), pp. 54–82.
12 D. Mathew, *The Celtic Peoples and Renaissance Europe* (1933), p. 64.
13 Trevor-Roper, op. cit., p. 109.
14 L. Guiney, *Recusant Poets* (1938), p. 305.
15 Ibid., p. 310.
16 M. Axton, 'The Queen's Two Bodies; Drama and the Elizabethan Succession', *RHS*, 1977, p. 92.
17 Guiney, op. cit., p. 310.
18 Ibid., p. 312.
19 Quoted M. Carrafiello, 'Robert Persons' Climate of Resistance and the Gunpowder Plot', *TSC*, 1988, p. 123.

Chapter Two

1 C. McIlwain, *The Political Works of James I*, Introduction (1918), liii.

2 G. Henry, *The Irish Military Community in Spanish Flanders, 1586–1621* (1992), p. 93.
3 E. St John Brooks, *Sir Christopher Hatton* (1946), p. 264.
4 Ibid., p. 268.
5 Henry, op. cit., p. 33.
6 Quoted C. Nicholl, *The Reckoning; The Murder of Christopher Marlowe* (1992), p. 237.
7 Ibid., p. 245.
8 D. Mathew, *Catholicism in England* (1955), p. 65.
9 M. Edmond, *Hilliard and Oliver, The Lives and Works of two great miniaturists* (1983), pp. 115–18.
10 L. Hotson, *I, William Shakespeare* (1937), pp. 146–7.
11 B.L. Harl. Mss 1974, f.21g.
12 A.H. Dodd, 'The Spanish Treason, the Gunpowder Plot, and the Catholic Refugees', *EHR*, LIII, 1938, p. 629.

Chapter Three

1 R. Mathias, *Whitsun Riot* (1963), pp. 122–3.
2 Ibid., p. 125.
3 M. Richings, *Espionage* (1934), p. 160.
4 R.W. Kenny, *Elizabeth's Admiral, The Political Career of Charles Howard, Earl of Nottingham 1536–1624* (1970), p. 263.
5 Mathias, op. cit., p. 126.
6 T.W. Laquer, 'Crowds, carnival and the state in English executions, 1604–1868', in A.L. Beier, D. Cannadine and J.M. Rosenhelm (eds), *Essays in English History in honour of Lawrence Stone* (1989), p. 327.
7 A.J. Loomie, 'Toleration and Diplomacy', *TAPS*, Vol, 53 pt 6, 1963, pp. 15–16.
8 Ibid., p. 19.
9 Carrafiello, op. cit., p. 127.
10 McIlwain, op. cit., xlviii.

11 S. Parnell Kerr, 'The Constable kept an Account', *N & Q* ns IV 1957, p. 168.
12 Dodd, op. cit., p. 639.
13 M. Nicholls, *Investigating Gunpowder Plot* (1991), p. 103.

Chapter Four

1 H. Belloc, *A History of England*, Vol. IV (1931), pp. 440–41.
2 F. Edwards, SJ, 'Still Investigating Gunpowder Plot', *RH*, 21, 3, 1993, p. 312.
3 J.W. Hales, *Notes and Essays on Shakespeare* (1884), p. 28.
4 Dodd, op. cit., p. 633.
5 J. Knipe, 'Conspiracy and Conscience; a psychological Study of the Gunpowder Plot', *The Churchman*, January 1930, p. 38.
6 Ibid., p. 39.
7 J. Gerard, SJ, *What was the Gunpowder Plot?* (1897), p. 9.
8 Nicholls, op. cit., p. 40.
9 Knipe, op. cit., p. 41.

Chapter Five

1 Hales, op. cit., p. 30.
2 Nicholls, op. cit., pp. 40–1.
3 O.F.G. Hogg, 'Gunpowder and its associations with the Crown', *JRA*, LXXI, 1944, p. 179.
4 S. Middelboe, 'Guy Certainly was Not Joking', *NCE*, 5 November 1987, p. 32.
5 Knipe, op. cit., p. 41.
6 Ibid., p. 43.
7 Ibid., p. 127, April 1930.
8 S.E. Sprott, 'Sir Edmund Baynham', *RH*, X, 1964, pp. 96–110.

Chapter Six

1 Haynes, op. cit., pp. 156–157.
2 Nicholls, op. cit., pp. 7–8; also G. Anstruther, 'Powder Treason', *Blackfriars*, xxxiii, 1952, p. 455.
3 Hales, op. cit., p. 31.
4 Knipe, op. cit., p. 130.
5 Ibid., p. 131.
6 Hales, op. cit., p. 42.
7 Knipe, op. cit., p. 133.
8 Ibid., p. 135.
9 Hales, op. cit., p. 44.
10 J. Wake, 'The Death of Francis Tresham', *NPP*, II, 1954, p. 32.
11 Hotson, op. cit., p. 190.

Chapter Seven

1 A. Haynes, *Robert Cecil, 1st Earl of Salisbury, Servant of Two Sovereigns* (1989), p. 153.
2 Edwards, *Investigating*, p. 323.
3 L. Winstanley, *Macbeth, King Lear and Contemporary History* (1922), p. 55.
4 Wake, op. cit., p. 33.
5 J. Wormald, 'Gunpowder, Treason and Scots', *JBS*, 24, 1985, p. 144.
6 Winstanley, op. cit., p. 44.
7 Wilson, *Monumental Brasses*, p. 272.
8 S.R. Gardiner, *History of England*, Vol. II, p. 234.
9 Nicholls, op. cit., p. 163.
10 *CSPV*, 1603–7, vol. 10, p. 293.

Chapter Eight

1 Hatfield MS 113/54.
2 J. Humphreys, 'The Wyntours of Huddington and the Gunpowder Plot', *TBMI*, xxx, 1904, p. 61.
3 Wilson, op. cit., p. 271.
4 Humphreys, op. cit., p. 63.
5 PRO, SP 14/216/22.
6 Humphreys, op. cit., p. 68.
7 *CSPD*, 1605, p. 271.
8 C. Breight, 'The Tempest and the Discourse of Treason', *Sh Q*, 41, 1 (1990), p. 2.
9 N. Lossky, *Lancelot Andrewes, the Preacher: The Origins of the Mystical Theology of the Church of England* (1991), p. 293.
10 H.N. Paul, *The Royal Play of Macbeth* (1950), p. 230.
11 L. Winstanley, op. cit., p. 44.
12 J. Wormald, op. cit., p. 164.
13 *CSPV*, 1603–7, vol. 10.

Chapter Nine

1 *Somer's Tracts*, Vol. xi, p. 113.
2 T. Longueville, *The Life of a Conspirator* (1895), p. 273.
3 A. Copley, *Another letter of Mr A.C. to his dis-Jesuited Kinsman* (1602).
4 *CSPD*, James I, Gunpowder Plot Book Pt II, n. 114.
5 T. Barlow, *The Gunpowder-Treason* (1679), reprinted 1850, p. 15.
6 Ibid., p. 59.
7 Longueville, op. cit., p. 288.
8 R.T. Peterson, *Sir Kenelm Digby, The Ornament of England, 1603–1665* (1956), p. 22.

9   Hales, op. cit., p. 49.
10 Peterson, op. cit., p. 23.
11 Wilson, *Monumental Brasses*, pp. 272–3.
12 Nicholls, op. cit., pp. 63–4.
13 Carrafiello, *Robert Parsons' Climate*, pp. 120–1.
14. Haynes, *Robert Cecil*, pp. 159–60.
15. J. Nichols (ed.), *The Progresses of King James I*, Vol. II (1828), pp. 38–43.
16. Paul, op. cit., pp. 238–9.
17. Ibid.
18. Lossky, op. cit., p. 289.
19. Ibid., p. 290.
20. H.R. Williamson, *Four Stuart Portraits* (1949), p. 67.

Chapter Ten

1   M. Axton, *The Queen's Two Bodies*, pp. 96–7.
2   Nicholls, op. cit., pp. 76–7.
3   A.L. Scoufos, *Shakespeare's typological satire* (1979), p. 290.
4   *CSPV*, 1603–7, vol. 10 p. 373.
5   H. Bowler, OSB, 'Sir Henry James Recusant (*c*. 1559–1625)', in A. Hollander and W. Kellaway (eds), *Studies in London History* (1969), pp. 289–312.
6   McIlwain, op. cit., li–liii.
7   Haynes, *Robert Cecil*, p. 189. Also D. Thomas, 'Financial and Administrative Developments', in H. Tomlinson (ed.), *Before the English Civil War: Essays in Early Stuart Politics and Government* (1983), pp. 104–5.

Chapter Eleven

1   C.J. Ryan, 'The Jacobean Oath of Allegiance, and English Lay Catholics, *CHR*, XXVIII, 2, 1942, p. 162.
2   Ibid., p. 163.
3   A. Boderie, *Ambassade de Monsieur de la Boderie* (1750, Paris), p. 121.
4   H. Foley (ed.), *Records of the English Provinces of the Society of Jesus*, IV (1873–8), p. 372.
5   Ryan, op. cit., p. 166.
6   L. Stone, *Family and Fortune; Studies in Aristocratic Finance in the Sixteenth and Seventeenth Centuries* (1973), pp. 197–8.
7   C.J. Sisson, *Lost Plays of Shakespeare's Age* (1936), pp. 4–5.
8   J.P. Collier, *Egerton Papers* (1840), pp. 453–4.
9   Ryan, op. cit., pp. 182–3.

Postlude

1   P. Yachnin, 'The Powerless Theatre' *ELR*, 21, 1, (1991), p. 69.
2   M. Bradbrook, *John Webster, Citizen and Dramatist* (1980), p. 120.
3   Yachnin, op. cit., p. 68.
4   Parry, 'Elizabeth in Jacobean London', *JMRS*, 23, 1 (1993), p. 105.
5   Yachnin, op. cit., p. 72.
6   D. Flynn, 'Donne and the Ancient Catholic Nobility', *ELR*, 19 (1989), p. 307.
7   Scoufos, op. cit., p. 291.
8   Hotson, op. cit., pp. 197–8.
9   S. Kozikowski, 'The Gowrie Conspiracy against James VI: A new source for Shakespeare's Macbeth, *Sh. S*, xiii (1980), p. 197.
10 Ibid.
11 H.L. Rogers, 'Double Profit' in *Macbeth* (1964), p. 48.
12 A.N. Stunz, 'The Date of Macbeth', *ELH*, ix (1942), pp. 97–8.
13 Winstanley, op. cit., p. 133.
14 Paul, op. cit.,
15 H.L. Rogers, 'An English Tailor and Father Garnet's Straw', *RES*, ns XVI, 1965, p. 48.
16 Gerard, op. cit., pp. 155–6.
17 Scoufos, op. cit., p. 286.
18 D. Cressy, *Bonfires and Bells, National memory and the Protestant calendar in Elizabethan and Stuart England* (1989), pp. 142–3.

Appendix I

1   K.J. Höltgen, *Aspects of the Emblem; Studies in the English Emblem Tradition and the European Context.*
2   I am very grateful to Ralph B. Weller for a long and detailed letter on Haydocke and the painting.

Appendix II

1   PRO, Sp 14/16. ff. 27–27v.
2   C. Blair, 'A Gunpowder Plotter's Sword?', *Handbook to the Eleventh Park Lane Arms Fair*, London, 1994, p. 2.
3   Ibid. p. 3. Also K. Stuber, *Waffen in Schweizerischen Landesmuseum*, 1980.
4   Blair, op. cit., p. 5.

Index

Christopher Wright   Iohn Wright